# More SCENES FROM SHAKESPEARE

## Twenty Cuttings for Acting and Directing Practice

D0814782

# MICHAEL WILSON

MERIWETHER PUBLISHING LTD.
Colorado Springs, Colorado

**Meriwether Publishing Ltd., Publisher**
P.O. Box 7710
Colorado Springs, CO 80933

**Executive editor: Theodore O. Zapel**
**Typesetting: Elisabeth Hendricks**
**Cover design: Janice Melvin**

© Copyright MCMXCIX Meriwether Publishing Ltd.
Printed in the United States of America
First Edition

**Library of Congress Cataloging-in-Publication Data**

Shakespeare, William, 1564-1616
    [Plays. Selections]
        More scenes from Shakespeare : twenty cuttings for acting and directing practice / [compiled by] Michael Wilson. -- 1st ed.
        p.   cm.
        Summary: A collection of twenty short scenes from six Shakespeare plays: "Macbeth," "Much Ado About Nothing," "A Midsummer Night's Dream," "King Lear," "As You Like It," and "The Taming of the Shrew." Each scene is preceded by a plot synopsis and descriptions of the characters.
        ISBN 1-56608-050-9
        1. Shakespeare, William, 1564-1616--Quotations. 2. Theater--Production and direction--Problems, exercises, etc. 3. Acting--Problems, exercises, etc. [1. Shakespeare, William, 1564-1616--Outlines, syllabi, etc. 2. Plays.] I. Wilson, Michael, 1952- II. Title.
  PR2771.W55   1999
  822.3'3--dc21

                                       98-55478
                                          CIP
                                         AC

1  2  3  4  5  6  7  8     03  02  01  00  99

*for*
*Sam*

*A scene from this book being performed by some of the author's students, including his son and daughter. From left to right, Sean McFadden, Shannan McFadden, Vanessa Wilson, and Jared Wilson.*

# *Personal Note from the Editor*

I was first introduced to Shakespeare in high school, and, quite frankly, I hated it. I remember sitting in sophomore English reading *Julius Caesar* out loud ... the only time I vaguely paid attention was during the assassination scene: I was chosen to read the part of Julius Caesar out loud to the class. As I stumbled through the lines, trying to understand anything that I was reading, embarrassing myself in front of my classmates, I finally breathed a heavy sigh of relief once I realized that I had been "killed." After I "died," I decided that since I was no longer among the living, I no longer needed to pay attention. Needless to say, I never understood a thing, did horribly on the test, and thus began my loathing of Shakespeare.

Things changed dramatically for me my freshman year of college. I attended Antelope Valley Junior College, and, to fulfill my fine arts requirement, I ended up taking a theater history course. The instructor was a young man by the name of Sam Anderson. He was different from any other instructor that I had ever had before: he was witty, caring, innovative, and slightly rebellious ... and he got me hooked on not only Shakespeare, but also theater, and, eventually, teaching. We studied *Othello* in class, and his readings and interpretations made the characters come alive — everything made sense! It was an absolute revelation to me: all of these strange words suddenly unfolded into this compelling story filled with extreme human emotions such as rage, jealousy, fear ... it was as if, to quote Blanche Dubois from *A Streetcar Named Desire*, "A blinding light appeared in the world that had always been half in shadow." (Pardon the dramatics, but that is how it appeared to me.) More importantly, Sam showed me the importance of good teaching, and how an excellent teacher can have such a positive effect on the lives of others.

Sam left teaching to pursue an acting career, and, as evidenced by his large body of work, has been tremendously successful. He has appeared as the elementary school principal in *Forrest Gump*, was Editor Gorpley in "Perfect Strangers," was Principal DeWitt on "Growing Pains," and can be seen often as the head cardiologist on "ER." In the vast scheme of things, his acting career has a broader impact than his teaching career did, but I often wonder how many more lives he would have molded had he remained a teacher. I often tell my students that I was incredibly fortunate to have him as my teacher and mentor, and that if I can only have half the success he had as a teacher, I will indeed be fulfilled.

Michael Wilson

# Acknowledgments

I would like to extend a sincere 'thank you' to the following people who, in one way or another, helped or influenced me in this project: my family, Celeste, Jared, and Vanessa Wilson; my mother and father, Chris and Ray Barnes; George and Joyce Cowie; Jim Watts; Wayne and Janet Stone;  Larry Parker (for all great influences and strength); Tim McFadden; Lee Terkelsen; Jeff Seaward; John Stockton, principal of Golden West High School; Sandy Warren, English Department Head; Bob Meier, Fine Arts Department Head; Sylvia Garoian (Stage Manager), Treasa Bonnar (Accompanist), and Paul Raheb (Vocal Music Instructor) — my cohorts in crime!! — and Steve Lamar, Paul Jones, and Noble Johnson of the College of Sequoias Theater Conservatory for their constant support and inspiration.

# Contents

# Introduction

I have been teaching high school theater for over eighteen years, and like other theater arts instructors, I am always looking for a better way to get my students excited about acting. I especially found it difficult covering Shakespeare or building a successful Shakespeare unit. Granted, several students would do very well and grasp the concepts, tone, subplots, and subtext, while others would struggle through the reading of an entire play.

A few years ago, I wrote *Scenes from Shakespeare: Fifteen Cuttings for the Classroom* to create a more successful (and more enjoyable) approach to Shakespeare. In the past, my drama classes would read an entire play, analyze the text, and select certain scenes to perform in class; this would take four to six weeks to complete, and, in the end, my students were "burned out." However, when I broke the plays into small, workable scenes, the students performed better, were more enthusiastic, and felt genuine success with the unit.

Here's how this book, like my previous one, works: I have chosen several scenes from various plays, making sure that they were relatively small in cast size. Each scene contains between two and seven characters. At the beginning of each scene, there is a list of characters (both lead and supporting), and, most importantly, a brief description of what has occurred thus far in the play. In other words, if a student is cast as Lady Macbeth, she can grasp the setting, the motivation, and the basic character development. Then, after enough rehearsal time, these scenes can be performed either in class or in competition. (Many of these scenes are excellent contest material.)

I did not, in this book, go into specific detail about the elements of subtext, such as tone, timing, pacing, actions, movement, and emphasis and progression; I feel that each teacher has his or her methods for doing so. I did give certain suggestions for character development, action, and scene dynamics, but if you are looking for sources on subtext, some excellent books are *How Tall Is this Ghost, John?*, by David Mallick and *Shakescenes*, by Russell Brown.

I have heard from several drama teachers who used my first book, and I was pleased to hear that they had better success teaching Shakespeare in this way than the conventional way of analyzing just one play.

I also met a professional Shakespearean actress from Ashland who told me she has used the book for "tune up" and acting practice.

Honestly, I feel the scenes from this book are more exciting to play and more interesting to watch than those in the first book. Shakespeare is truly amazing: the conflicts, the emotions, the jealousies, and the passions make his work exciting, and, realistically, quite relevant in today's world.

## A Note to the Acting Student

For those who are relative beginners, let me give you some quick helpful hints on how to approach the acting of Shakespeare:

• First of all, don't let the language intimidate you. Remember, these lines were written for actors to perform. Some of my students have taken their characters and broken them down into small sections, analyzing each section for movement, motivation, and character development.

• Make sure you fully understand each phrase and each word. As you read your lines, it is imperative to comprehend the meaning of what you are saying and why you are saying it.

• When committing lines to memory, again, work in sections, memorizing each separately and piecing them together as you go. One way to memorize easier is to write your lines out in paragraph form; this will also help you get over the barrier of saying your lines in poetic verse. By doing this, you will also start to see a definite rhythm, a meter, and you will see the logical places for emphasis and for pausing.

• When rehearsing, make notes in the margins of your script. Write any blocking and movement notes, underline words that need to be emphasized, make notes for pausing. These notes will also help you memorize your lines more quickly, because you will begin to associate your lines with your movement: it becomes logical, understandable, and easier to develop your character to an honest and believable depth.

• When speaking your lines, speak them honestly. Pacing and dynamics are crucial; if you say your lines too flatly, you will lose interest and the interest of your audience; if you overact and approach your character with too much intensity, there is no place for your character to go. Remember this: justified pausing is a great way to create tension and tone. However, pausing must be used sparingly and in the exact context.

Once you have discovered Shakespeare's characters and their conflicts, passions, and lives, I hope you will develop an appreciation for the genius of the Bard. As previously stated, his work is as relevant today as it was 300 years ago, and students will, no doubt, be analyzing his work for centuries to come.

# Macbeth
## Act I, Scene 2

**Characters:** Duncan, Malcolm, Sergeant, Ross

**Extras:** Lennox, Angus

The storyline unfolds in eleventh-century Scotland under the leadership of King Duncan. In the previous scene, the famous "witches scene," the tone of the play was established: three ugly, cackling witches are gathered in a thunderstorm howling over their evil plans. It is important to note that the audiences in Shakespeare's time did believe in witches; even those who scoffed at their existence were unsure, from time to time, of their own beliefs in them.

Shakespeare wrote *Macbeth* in approximately 1605 to please King James I, who had a fascination with the supernatural. According to Paul R. Jones, theater arts instructor at the College of Sequoias, "Not to be confused with devil worship, witches have no power over human action, only that of wind and water. They also have the power to prophesy. Macbeth is a willing victim of prophecy."

With all of this in mind, it is sufficient to say that the play begins with a sense, or tone, if you will, of doom; the three witches are planning their next meeting, one which will include Macbeth. Because of the lightning and thunder and foreboding sense of mystery, many critics and scholars believe that the play opens in the middle of chaos, as the witches "hover through the fog and filthy air."

However, the following scene (Act I, Scene 2) is quite a contrast in both tone and spirit from the previous one. Furthermore, there is a genuine sense of immediacy in this scene. A sergeant, bleeding from wounds just received in battle, stumbles into the camp of King Duncan and informs him how Macbeth, a general in his army, has killed the King's enemy, the rebellious Macdonwald; the Thane (Lord) of Ross later enters and states that Macbeth combined his forces with those of Banquo, another general in King Duncan's army, and together conquered the Thane of Cawdor and the King of Norway; as a resulting term of peace, the King of Norway agreed to pay them a handsome sum:

> "Nor would we deign him burial of his men
> Till he disbursed at Saint Colme's inch\*
> Ten thousand dollars to our general use."

While playing this scene, emphasis must be placed on the immediacy of both time and place. They are close to the center of the battlefield, as evidenced by the sergeant's fresh wounds and blood; please keep in mind this scene's primary purpose, which is to inform King Duncan (and the audience as well) of the current situation and developments in the battle. Play it with urgency, keep the tempo and rhythm of the scene dynamic, yet don't lose the essence of the characters and plot by delivering your lines too quickly. The sergeant, though bleeding from wounds received in the fighting, reflects honest heroism and loyalty to Duncan; note too that as the news reaches the King about the defeat of his enemies, the King changes his demeanor from concern of the battle:

> "What bloody man is that? He can report,
> As seemeth by his plight, of the revolt
> The newest state ...
> O, valiant cousin! worthy gentleman!"

to giving the order to execute the Thane of Cawdor and bequeathing that title to the victorious Macbeth:

> "No more that thane of Cawdor shall deceive
> Our bosom interest: go pronounce his present death,
> And with his former title greet Macbeth."

This scene also prepares the way for Scene 3 to unfold with the meeting of the witches and Macbeth and Banquo. It is also interesting to note that the man whom King Duncan considers to be the hero in this bloody battle will be his murderer later in the play.

*(Despite the fact that the reference for Act I, Scene 1 is very important, I omitted it strictly because it is only 30-45 seconds long. This book is to be used primarily for acting practice and for use in the classroom, and the parts in that particular scene are too short to warrant honest and lengthy criticism. However, it is necessary for the actors to read and be familiar with that scene to understand and appreciate Shakespeare's tone and brooding sense of atmosphere.)*

\*Saint Colme's inch: Inchcolm, the Isle of St. Columba, in the Firth of Forth.

1   *SETTING:* A camp near Forres. Alarum.
2   *AT RISE:* Enter KING DUNCAN, MALCOLM, DONALBAIN,
3       LENNOX, with attendants, meeting a bleeding SERGEANT.
4
5   **DUNCAN: What bloody man is that? He can report,**
6       **As seemeth by his plight, of the revolt**
7       **The newest state.**
8   **MALCOLM: This is the sergeant,**
9       **Who like a good and hardy soldier fought**
10      **'Gainst my captivity ... Hail, brave friend!**
11      **Say to the king the knowledge of the broil**
12      **As thou didst leave it.**
13   **SERGEANT: Doubtful it stood;**
14      **As two spent swimmers that do cling together**
15      **And choke their art ... The merciless Macdonwald —**
16      **Worthy to be a rebel, for to that**
17      **The multiplying villainies of nature**
18      **Do swarm upon him — from the Western Isles**
19      **Of kerns and gallowglasses is supplied;**
20      **And Fortune, on his damned quarrel smiling,**
21      **Showed like a rebel's whore: but all's too weak:**
22      **For brave Macbeth — well he deserves that name —**
23      **Disdaining fortune, with his brandished steel,**
24      **Which smoked with bloody execution,**
25      **Like Valour's minion carved out his passage**
26      **Till he faced the slave;**
27      **Which ne'er shook hands, nor bade farewell to him,**
28      **Till he unseamed him from the nave to the chops,**
29      **And fixed his head upon our battlements.**
30   **DUNCAN: O, valiant cousin! worthy gentleman!**
31   **SERGEANT: As whence the sun 'gins his reflection**
32      **Shipwracking storms and direful thunders break;**
33      **So from that spring whence comfort seemed to come**
34      **Discomfort swells. Mark, king of Scotland, mark!**
35      **No sooner justice had, with valour armed,**

| | |
|---|---|
| 1 | Compelled these skipping kerns to trust their heels, |
| 2 | But the Norweyan lord, surveying vantage, |
| 3 | With furbished arms and new supplies of men, |
| 4 | Began a fresh assault. |
| 5 | DUNCAN:  Dismayed not this |
| 6 | Our captains, Macbeth and Banquo? |
| 7 | SERGEANT: Yes; as sparrows, eagles; or the hare, the lion; |
| 8 | If I say sooth, I must report they were |
| 9 | As cannons overcharged with double cracks, |
| 10 | So they doubly redoubled strokes upon the foe: |
| 11 | Except they meant to bathe in reeking wounds, |
| 12 | Or memorize another Golgotha, |
| 13 | I cannot tell: |
| 14 | But I am faint, my gashes cry for help. |
| 15 | DUNCAN: So well thy words become thee, as thy wounds; |
| 16 | They smack of honour both. Go get him surgeons. |
| 17 | *(Exit SERGEANT with attendants.)* |
| 18 | Who comes here? *(Enter ROSS and ANGUS.)* |
| 19 | MALCOLM: The worthy thane of Ross. |
| 20 | LENNOX: What a haste looks through his eyes! So should |
| 21 | he look |
| 22 | That seems to speak things strange. |
| 23 | ROSS: God save the king! |
| 24 | DUNCAN: Whence cam'st thou, worthy thane? |
| 25 | ROSS: From Fife, great king, |
| 26 | Where the Norweyan banners flout the sky, |
| 27 | And fan our people cold. |
| 28 | Norway himself, with terrible numbers, |
| 29 | Assisted by that most disloyal traitor |
| 30 | The thane of Cawdor, began a dismal conflict, |
| 31 | Till that Bellona's bridegroom, lapped in proof, |
| 32 | Confronted him with self-comparisons, |
| 33 | Point against point, rebellious arm 'gainst arm, |
| 34 | Curbing his lavish spirit: and, to conclude, |
| 35 | The victory fell on us. |

1    DUNCAN:  Great happiness!

2    ROSS:  That now

3          Sweno, the Norways' king, craves composition;

4          Nor would we deign him burial of his men

5          Till he disbursed, at Saint Colme's Inch,

6          Ten thousand dollars to our general use.

7    DUNCAN:  No more that thane of Cawdor shall deceive

8          Our bosom interest: go pronounce his present death,

9          And with his former title greet Macbeth.

10   ROSS:  I'll see it done.

11   DUNCAN:  What he hath lost, noble Macbeth hath won.

12   *(Exit all.)*

13

14

15

16

17

18

19

20

21

22

23

24

25

26

27

28

29

30

31

32

33

34

35

# Macbeth
## Act I, Scene 3

**Characters:** Three Witches, Macbeth, Banquo
**Supporting Characters:** Ross, Angus

This scene opens on a heath with the witches meeting again as agreed upon in Scene 1. (It is worthy to note that the heath, according to Shakespeare's settings, symbolizes an environment that is unproductive, deserted, and unfriendly.) As the witches prepare their magic spells, one including the punishment of a sailor because his wife would not share her chestnuts with one of them, their meeting is interrupted by the arrival of Macbeth and Banquo.

Macbeth and Banquo are two generals in the army of King Duncan of Scotland and are returning home from a victorious battle with the King of Norway. Macbeth's current title is Thane (Lord) of Glamis; after his recent victory over the King of Norway, Duncan deemed him with the title Thane of Cawdor, but he has yet to hear of this honor.

Returning from battle, Macbeth and Banquo see the three witches and begin conversing with them. The witches greet Macbeth and startle him by acknowledging him with his current title "Thane of Glamis," his soon-to-be-position of "Thane of Cawdor," and, finally, as the "King Hereafter." Stunned, amused, and intrigued by this prophesy, Banquo asks the witches to tell him about his future. Their response, indeed, is puzzling: "Lesser than Macbeth, and greater."

Macbeth questions the witches about their prophesy, but they vanish without explanation. As Macbeth and Banquo discuss the strange prediction they have heard, Ross and Angus enter and deliver the news that Macbeth indeed is to become the Thane of Cawdor. Banquo is amazed that the witches' prediction of Macbeth's second title has come true. ("What, can the devil speak true?") This event, for the most part, marks a culmination in Macbeth's life: he is a soldier and a general and has risen in the ranks as far as he can go; in other words, he has reached the end of his dream, a plateau, if you will. The words from the witches not only confuse him, but they inspire him ... he is a general, the Thane of Glamis, now the Thane of Cawdor, and, perhaps, someday ... a king? (Remember the prophecy of King Hereafter.)

It is then that Macbeth delivers his soliloquy, one whose importance cannot be overlooked. He goes into almost a trance-like state and verbalizes his desire for power; he first asks Banquo if he hopes that his (Banquo's) descendants will become kings. Banquo responds by stating that though the prophesies sound tempting and pleasurable, they could cause trouble.

Macbeth delivers his fate to the audience: he is contemplating his future in becoming the King of Scotland. He could, as it were, leave it to fate and receive the crown by chance. But moreover, the thought of murdering Duncan to gain access to the crown is what draws him into this hypnotic state:

"... Why do I yield to that suggestion
Whose horrid image doth unfix my hair,
And make my seated heart knock at my ribs,
Against the use of nature? Present fears
Are less than horrible imaginings:
My thought, whose murder yet is but fantastical,
Shakes so my single state of man that function
Is smothered in surmise, and nothing is
But what is not." (Page 15 lines 13-21)

He is, in essence, foretelling his own fate: nothing, including any battle he has previously fought, will be as frightening as the fear he will experience after he decides to murder the king. As a result, he will become tormented and confused, burdened with guilt of consciousness. It is this state of mind that will forever cloud his judgment of upcoming events.

After his soliloquy, Banquo dismisses Macbeth's trance-like state to Ross and Angus as his (Macbeth's) inability to grasp the gravity and importance of his newly anointed position. Macbeth responds,

"... My dull brain was wrought
With things forgotten. Kind gentlemen, your pains
Are registered where every day I turn
The leaf to read them."
This, of course, can be interpreted as a passive statement or can be construed as ironic understatement.

1   *SETTING:* A heath. Thunder.
2   *AT RISE:* Enter the three WITCHES.
3
4   **FIRST WITCH:  Where hast thou been, sister?**
5   **SECOND WITCH:  Killing swine.**
6   **THIRD WITCH:  Sister, where thou?**
7   **FIRST WITCH:  A sailor's wife had chestnuts in her lap,**
8        **And munched, and munched, and munched: "Give me,"**
9         **quoth I.**
10       **"Aroint thee, witch!" the rump-fed ronyon cries.**
11       **Her husband's to Aleppo gone, master o' th' Tiger:**
12       **But in a sieve I'll thither sail,**
13       **And, like a rat without a tail,**
14       **I'll do, I'll do, and I'll do.**
15   **SECOND WITCH:  I'll give thee a wind.**
16   **FIRST WITCH:  Th'art kind.**
17   **THIRD WITCH:  And I another.**
18   **FIRST WITCH:  I myself have all the other,**
19       **And the very ports they blow,**
20       **All the quarters that they know**
21       **I'th' shipman's card.**
22       **I will drain him dry as hay:**
23       **Sleep shall neither night nor day**
24       **Hang upon his pent-house lid;**
25       **He shall live a man forbid:**
26       **Weary se'nights nine times nine**
27       **Shall he dwindle, peak, and pine:**
28       **Though his bark cannot be lost,**
29       **Yet it shall be tempest-tost.**
30       **Look what I have.**
31   **SECOND WITCH:  Show me, show me.**
32   **FIRST WITCH:  Here I have a pilot's thumb,**
33       **Wrecked as homeward he did come.**
34   **THIRD WITCH:  *(Sound of drum)* A drum, a drum!**
35       **Macbeth doth come.**

1   ALL:  The Weird Sisters, hand in hand,
2         Posters of the sea and land,
3         Thus do go, about, about,
4         Thrice to thine, and thrice to mine,
5         And thrice again, to make up nine.
6         Peace! the charm's wound up.
7         *(Enter MACBETH and BANQUO.)*
8   MACBETH:  So foul and fair a day I have not seen.
9   BANQUO:  How far is't called to Forres? What are these,
10       So withered, and so wild in their attire,
11       That look not like th'inhabitants o'th' earth,
12       And yet are on't? Live you? or are you aught
13       That man may question? You seem to understand me,
14       By each at once her choppy finger laying
15       Upon her skinny lips: you should be women,
16       And yet your beards forbid me to interpret
17       That you are so.
18   MACBETH:  Speak, if you can: what are you?
19   FIRST WITCH:  All hail, Macbeth! hail to thee, thane of
20       Glamis!
21   SECOND WITCH:  All hail, Macbeth! hail to thee, thane of
22       Cawdor!
23   THIRD WITCH:  All hail, Macbeth! that shalt be king
24       hereafter.
25   BANQUO:  Good sir, why do you start, and seem to fear
26       Things that do sound so fair? I'th' name of truth,
27       Are ye fantastical, or that indeed
28       Which outwardly ye show? My noble partner
29       You greet with present grace and great prediction
30       Of noble having and of royal hope,
31       That he seems rapt withall: to me you speak not.
32       If you can look into the seeds of time,
33       And say which grain will grow and which will not,
34       Speak then to me, who neither beg nor fear
35       Your favours nor your hate.

1   **FIRST WITCH: Hail!**
2   **SECOND WITCH: Hail!**
3   **THIRD WITCH: Hail!**
4   **FIRST WITCH: Lesser than Macbeth, and greater.**
5   **SECOND WITCH: Not so happy, yet much happier.**
6   **THIRD WITCH: Thou shalt get kings, though thou be none:**
7   **So all hail, Macbeth and Banquo!**
8   **FIRST WITCH: Banquo and Macbeth, all hail!**
9   **MACBETH: Stay, you imperfect speakers, tell me more:**
10   **By Sinel's death I know I am thane of Glamis;**
11   **But how of Cawdor? the thane of Cawdor lives**
12   **A prosperous gentleman; and to be king**
13   **Stands not within the prospect of belief,**
14   **No more than to be Cawdor. Say from whence**
15   **You owe this strange intelligence, or why**
16   **Upon this blasted heath you stop our way**
17   **With such prophetic greeting? Speak, I charge you.**
18   *(They vanish.)*
19   **BANQUO: The earth hath bubbles, as the water has,**
20   **And these are of them: whither are they vanished?**
21   **MACBETH: Into the air; and what seemed corporal, melted,**
22   **As breath into the wind. Would they had stayed!**
23   **BANQUO: Were such things here as we do speak about?**
24   **Or have we eaten on the insane root**
25   **That takes the reason prisoner?**
26   **MACBETH: Your children shall be kings.**
27   **BANQUO: You shall be king.**
28   **MACBETH: And thane of Cawdor too: went it not so?**
29   **BANQUO: To th' selfsame tune and words. Who's here?**
30   *(Enter ROSS and ANGUS.)*
31   **ROSS: The king hath happily received, Macbeth,**
32   **The news of thy success: and when he reads**
33   **Thy personal venture in the rebels' fight,**
34   **His wonders and his praises do contend**
35   **Which should be thine or his: silenced with that,**

13

| 1 | In viewing o'er the rest o'th' selfsame day, |
|---|---|
| 2 | He finds thee in the stout Norweyan ranks, |
| 3 | Nothing afeard of what thyself didst make |
| 4 | Strange images of death. As thick as hail |
| 5 | Came post with post, and every one did bear |
| 6 | Thy praises in his kingdom's great defence, |
| 7 | And poured them down before him. |
| 8 | ANGUS: We are sent |
| 9 | To give thee from our royal master thanks, |
| 10 | Only to herald thee into his sight, |
| 11 | Not pay thee. |
| 12 | ROSS: And for an earnest of a greater honour, |
| 13 | He bade me, from him, call thee thane of Cawdor: |
| 14 | In which addition, hail, most worthy thane, |
| 15 | For it is thine. |
| 16 | BANQUO: *(Aside)* What, can the devil speak true? |
| 17 | MACBETH: The thane of Cawdor lives: why do you dress me |
| 18 | In borrowed robes? |
| 19 | ANGUS: Who was the thane lives yet, |
| 20 | But under heavy judgment bears that life |
| 21 | Which he deserves to lose. Whether he was combined |
| 22 | With those of Norway, or did line the rebel |
| 23 | With hidden help and vantage, or that with both |
| 24 | He laboured in his country's wreck, I know not; |
| 25 | But treasons capital, confessed, and proved, |
| 26 | Have overthrown him. |
| 27 | MACBETH: *(Aside)* Glamis, and thane of Cawdor: |
| 28 | The greatest is behind. Thanks for your pains — |
| 29 | *(To BANQUO)* Do you not hope your children shall be |
| 30 | kings, |
| 31 | When those that gave the thane of Cawdor to me |
| 32 | Promised no less to them? |
| 33 | BANQUO: *(To MACBETH)* That, trusted home, |
| 34 | Might yet enkindle you unto the crown, |
| 35 | Besides the thane of Cawdor. But 'tis strange: |

| | |
|---|---|
| 1 | And oftentimes, to win us to our harm, |
| 2 | The instruments of darkness tell us truths, |
| 3 | Win us with honest trifles, to betray's |
| 4 | In deepest consequence. |
| 5 | Cousins, a word, I pray you. |
| 6 | MACBETH: *(Aside)* Two truths are told, |
| 7 | As happy prologues to the swelling act |
| 8 | Of the imperial theme. I thank you, gentlemen. |
| 9 | This supernatural soliciting |
| 10 | Cannot be ill; cannot be good. If ill, |
| 11 | Why hath it given me earnest of success, |
| 12 | Commencing in a truth? I am Thane of Cawdor. |
| 13 | If good, why do I yield to that suggestion |
| 14 | Whose horrid image doth unfix my hair, |
| 15 | And make my seated heart knock at my ribs, |
| 16 | Against the use of nature? Present fears |
| 17 | Are less than horrible imaginings: |
| 18 | My thought, whose murder yet is but fantastical, |
| 19 | Shakes so my single state of man that function |
| 20 | Is smothered in surmise, and nothing is |
| 21 | But what is not. |
| 22 | BANQUO: Look how our partner's rapt. |
| 23 | MACBETH: *(Aside)* If chance will have me king, why, |
| 24 | chance may crown me, |
| 25 | Without my stir. |
| 26 | BANQUO: New honours come upon him, |
| 27 | Like our strange garments, cleave not to their mould |
| 28 | But with the aid of use. |
| 29 | MACBETH: Come what come may, |
| 30 | Time and the hour runs through the roughest day. |
| 31 | BANQUO: Worthy Macbeth, we stay upon your leisure. |
| 32 | MACBETH: Give me your favour: my dull brain was wrought |
| 33 | With things forgotten. Kind gentlemen, your pains |
| 34 | Are registered where every day I turn |
| 35 | The leaf to read them … Let us toward the king. |

| | |
|---|---|
| 1 | Think upon what hath chanced: and at more time, |
| 2 | The interim having weighed it, let us speak |
| 3 | Our free hearts each to other. |
| 4 | BANQUO:  Very gladly. |
| 5 | MACBETH:  Till then, enough. Come, friends. *(Exit all.)* |
| 6 | |
| 7 | |
| 8 | |
| 9 | |
| 10 | |
| 11 | |
| 12 | |
| 13 | |
| 14 | |
| 15 | |
| 16 | |
| 17 | |
| 18 | |
| 19 | |
| 20 | |
| 21 | |
| 22 | |
| 23 | |
| 24 | |
| 25 | |
| 26 | |
| 27 | |
| 28 | |
| 29 | |
| 30 | |
| 31 | |
| 32 | |
| 33 | |
| 34 | |
| 35 | |

# Macbeth
## Act I, Scene 7

**Characters:** Macbeth, Lady Macbeth

As previously noted, the play takes place in eleventh-century Scotland under the rule of King Duncan. Macbeth, a general in the King's army, has recently been victorious in battle and has risen high in the ranks; as a matter of fact, he has ascended as far as he can: in other words, he has reached the end of his dream. However, his lust for ambition makes him contemplate the possibilities of his future — he can receive the crown of Scotland by chance, or he can plan to murder the king. (refer to Act I, Scene 3)

In this scene, Macbeth is in a room in the castle and is debating with himself whether he will kill Duncan or not. As we see, there are many reasons for not committing the murder. First of all, he wishes that the murder could happen quickly and with little reaction or after-effects from the subjects. This is highly unlikely, because Duncan is a much-loved king, and therefore the assassination would be risky. Duncan's enormous popularity is shown:

"… Besides, this Duncan
Hath borne his faculties so meek, hath been
So clear in his great office, that his virtues
Will plead like angels, trumpet-tongued, against
The deep damnation of his taking-off;
And pity, like a naked newborn babe,
Striding the blast, or heaven's cherubin horsed
Upon the sightless couriers of the air,
Shall blow the horrid deed in every eye,
That tears shall drown the wind." (Page 20 lines 20-29)

Also, Macbeth fears the consequence of eternal damnation, of punishment in the afterlife:

"… If th' assassination

17

> Could trammel up the consequence, and catch
> With his surcease success; that but this blow
> Might be the be-all and end-all here,
> But here, upon this bank and shoal of time,
> We'd jump the life to come." (Page 20 lines 6-11)

We soon realize that these fears do not weigh as heavily with Macbeth as do the immediate ones. How will Macbeth's new subjects react? How could he complete a murder so perfectly that he could escape any punishment? Most importantly, Duncan is enormously popular with his subjects. If he succeeds, he knows that his offense of murdering his king will somehow "return to plague" him.

With all of this in mind, he realizes that it is only his ambition that is driving him to meditate about the murder, and, as a result, changes his mind and "alters his course," so to speak:

> "… I have no spur
> To prick the sides of my intent, but only
> Vaulting ambition, which o'erleaps itself
> And falls on th' other —" (Page 20 lines 29-32)

However, his decision not to murder Duncan is changed with the arrival of Lady Macbeth, and it is important to mention a few words about her. She is indeed one of Shakespeare's most interesting women characters, and according to Thomas Marc Parrott, professor of English at Princeton University, "Lady Macbeth is no monster of cruelty nor demon of ambition … It is plain that Shakespeare conceived her as a slight and delicate woman … She is ambitious, indeed, but solely for her husband … The dominant note in her character is an imperious and masterful will. Intensely practical, she has none of Macbeth's fears and scruples. Her final ruin is not due to remorse, but to a complete collapse of body and mind brought on by the strain which she had suffered and the crushing disappointment of her hopes."

It is indeed her will that changes Macbeth's mind to go forth with the plan to murder Duncan. Her argument with Macbeth is a clever one: because he is a general and a warrior, she strikes him in his most vulnerable area — his courage, and, inevitably, his manhood:

"… Art thou afeard
To be the same in thine own act and valour
As thou art in desire? Wouldst thou have that
Which thou esteem'st the ornament of life,
And live a coward in thine own esteem."
(Page 21 lines 12-16)
She also gives a shocking image to demonstrate her loyalty to
him and loyalty to the task of the murder itself:
"… I have given suck, and know
How tender 'tis to love the babe that milks me —
I would, while it was smiling in my face,
Have plucked my nipple from his boneless gums,
And dashed the brains out, had I so sworn as you
Have done to this." (Page 21 lines 29-34)
As a result of her persuasive speech, Macbeth finds new courage
within himself. He agrees to his wife's plan: they will offer wine to Duncan's guards and murder the king while he is asleep in his chamber.

1    ***SETTING:*** Macbeth's castle.
2    ***AT RISE:*** Enter a SEWER directing diverse servants. Then
3    enter MACBETH.
4
5    **MACBETH: If it were done, when 'tis done, then 'twere well**
6         **It were done quickly: if th' assassination**
7         **Could trammel up the consequence, and catch,**
8         **With his surcease, success; that but this blow**
9         **Might be the be-all and the end-all here,**
10       **But here, upon this bank and shoal of time,**
11       **We'd jump the life to come. But in these cases**
12       **We still have judgment here: that we but teach**
13       **Blood instructions, which being taught return**
14       **To plague th'inventor: this even-handed justice**
15       **Commends th'ingredience of our poisoned chalice**
16       **To our own lips. He's here in double trust:**
17       **First, as I am his kinsman and his subject,**
18       **Strong both against the deed: then, as his host,**
19       **Who should against his murderer shut the door,**
20       **Not bear the knife myself. Besides this Duncan**
21       **Hath borne his faculties so meek, hath been**
22       **So clear in his great office, that his virtues**
23       **Will plead like angels, trumpet-tongued, against**
24       **The deep damnation of his taking-off;**
25       **And pity, like a naked newborn babe,**
26       **Striding the blast, or Heaven's cherubin, horsed**
27       **Upon the sightless couriers of the air,**
28       **Shall blow the horrid deed in every eye,**
29       **That tears shall drown the wind. I have no spur**
30       **To prick the sides of my intent, but only**
31       **Vaulting ambition, which o'erleaps itself,**
32       **And falls on th'other** — *(Enter LADY MACBETH.)*
33       **How now! what news?**
34    **LADY MACBETH: He has almost supped: why have you**
35         **left the chamber?**

1   MACBETH: Hath he asked for me?
2   LADY MACBETH: Know you not he has?
3   MACBETH: We will proceed no further in this business:
4         He hath honoured me of late, and I have bought
5         Golden opinions from all sorts of people,
6         Which would be worn now in their newest gloss,
7         Not cast aside so soon.
8   LADY MACBETH: Was the hope drunk
9         Wherein you dressed yourself? hath it slept since?
10        And wakes it now, to look so green and pale
11        At what it did so freely? From this time
12        Such I account thy love. Art thou afeard
13        To be the same in thine own act and valour
14        As thou art in desire? Wouldst thou have that
15        Which thou esteem'st the ornament of life,
16        And live a coward in thine own esteem,
17        Letting "I dare not" wait upon "I would",
18        Like the poor cat i'th'adage?
19   MACBETH: Prithee, peace:
20        I dare do all that may become a man;
21        Who dares do more is none.
22   LADY MACBETH: What beast was't then
23        That made you break this enterprise to me?
24        When you durst do it, then you were a man;
25        And, to be more than what you were, you would
26        Be so much more the man. Nor time nor place
27        Did then adhere, and yet you would make both:
28        They have made themselves, and that their fitness now
29        Does unmake you. I have given suck, and know
30        How tender 'tis to love the babe that milks me —
31        I would, while it was smiling in my face,
32        Have plucked my nipple from his boneless gums,
33        And dashed the brains out, had I so sworn as you
34        Have done to this.
35   MACBETH: If we should fail?

| | |
|---|---|
| 1 | LADY MACBETH:  We fail? |
| 2 | But screw your courage to the sticking place, |
| 3 | And we'll not fail. When Duncan is asleep — |
| 4 | Whereto the rather shall his day's hard journey |
| 5 | Soundly invite him — his two chamberlains |
| 6 | Will I with wine and wassail so convince, |
| 7 | That memory, the warder of the brain, |
| 8 | Shall be a fume, and the receipt of reason |
| 9 | A limbec only: when in swinish sleep |
| 10 | Their drenched natures lie as in a death, |
| 11 | What cannot you and I perform upon |
| 12 | Th'unguarded Duncan? what not put upon |
| 13 | His spongy officers, who shall bear the guilt |
| 14 | Or our great quell? |
| 15 | MACBETH:  Bring forth men-children only! |
| 16 | For thy undaunted mettle should compose |
| 17 | Nothing but males. Will it not be received, |
| 18 | When we have marked with blood those sleepy two |
| 19 | Of his own chamber, and used their very daggers, |
| 20 | That they have done't? |
| 21 | LADY MACBETH:  Who dares receive it other, |
| 22 | As we shall make our griefs and clamour roar |
| 23 | Upon his death? |
| 24 | MACBETH:  I am settled, and bend up |
| 25 | Each corporal agent to this terrible feat. |
| 26 | Away, and mock the time with fairest show: |
| 27 | False face must hide what the false heart doth know. |
| 28 | *(Exit.)* |
| 29 | |
| 30 | |
| 31 | |
| 32 | |
| 33 | |
| 34 | |
| 35 | |

# Macbeth
## Act II, Scene 2

**Characters:** Lady Macbeth, Macbeth

This is an exciting scene to play because of its dynamics and pacing. It also reflects how Shakespeare could portray a myriad of emotions in such a short space of time, reflecting the dramatic setting of the murder of a popular king and the very human reactions of guilt, remorse, and fear of the murderer(s).

Here is what has happened thus far: Macbeth, a general in King Duncan's army in eleventh-century Scotland, has just murdered his king. He did so for various reasons; he has climbed the ranks of the army quickly and can go no higher; except to the level of king. In a previous scene, he decides not to go forth with the plan to murder, but is persuaded by his wife, Lady Macbeth, to resume his "course of fate" and kill the king. (Refer to Act I, Scene 7.)

This scene unfolds immediately after the murder. Lady Macbeth's plan was for Macbeth to drug two guards outside King Duncan's chamber with wine, sneak into the room, kill the king, and place the bloody daggers into the hands of the guards, thereby making them appear as the murderers.

The scene opens with Lady Macbeth nervously pacing. She is startled by the cry of an owl and by the tolling of a bell, which is Shakespeare's reference to the nearby Newgate Prison (where they would ring a bell before a prisoner would be executed).

Macbeth enters. He has just butchered King Duncan, and his hands and daggers are bathed in blood. Note the dialog between the two, which is fast paced and irregular, some critics suggesting that it reflects the beating of a racing heart. Note also how their nervousness makes them seem feeble yet strangely human; remember that Macbeth is indeed a very powerful figure in Scotland, yet it is his wife, Lady Macbeth, who emerges strong here.

Macbeth is overwhelmed with fear, guilt, and remorse:
"I am afraid to think what I have done;
Look on't again I dare not." (Page 26 lines 33-34)
But Lady Macbeth's sense of purpose and practicality take over. She instructs him to wash his hands of the blood and place the bloody daggers in the hands of the drugged guards. When Macbeth's confusion rends him helpless, Lady Macbeth snaps at him and says she'll complete the deed herself:
"Infirm of purpose!
Give me the daggers: the sleeping and the dead
Are but as pictures: 'tis the eye of childhood
That fears a painted devil. If he do bleed,
I'll gild the faces of the grooms withal,
For it must seem their guilt." (Page 27 lines 1-6)
Alone, Macbeth becomes lost in worry and guilt. He thinks of his wife's command of washing the blood from his hands and says:
"Will all great Neptune's ocean wash this blood
Clean from my hand? No; this my hand will rather
The multitudinous seas incarnadine,
Making the green one red." (Page 27 lines 10-13)
Lady Macbeth's firmness and control is shown again upon her return. She assures Macbeth that they won't get caught if they simply follow their plan. ("A little water clears us of this deed; how easy it is then!") But even as she speaks, there is a loud knocking at the gates, disturbing any chance they have for a momentary peace. She then instructs her husband to put on his nightgown and act like nothing is wrong; but Macbeth's final words in this scene show us that, for him, that will be easier said than done.

1    ***SETTING:*** The hall of the castle of MACBETH.
2    ***AT RISE:*** LADY MACBETH enters.
3
4    LADY MACBETH:  That which hath made them drunk
5            hath made me bold:
6            What hath quenched them hath given me fire. Hark! Peace!
7            It was the owl that shrieked, the fatal bellman,
8            Which gives the stern'st good-night. He is about it:
9            The doors are open; and the surfeited grooms
10           Do mock their charge with snores: I have drugged their
11           possetts,
12           That death and nature do contend about them,
13           Whether they live or die.
14   MACBETH:  *(Off-stage)* Who's there? what, ho!
15   LADY MACBETH:  Alack! I am afraid they have awaked,
16           And 'tis not done: th'attempt and not the deed
17           Confounds us. Hark! I laid their daggers ready,
18           He could not miss 'em. Had he not resembled
19           My father as he slept, I had done't. *(Enter MACBETH.)*
20           My husband!
21   MACBETH:  I have done the deed. Didst thou not hear a noise?
22   LADY MACBETH: I heard the owl scream, and the crickets cry.
23           Did you not speak?
24   MACBETH:  When?
25   LADY MACBETH:  Now.
26   MACBETH:  As I descended?
27   LADY MACBETH:  Ay.
28   MACBETH:  Hark!
29           Who lies i'th' second chamber?
30   LADY MACBETH:  Donalbain.
31   MACBETH:  This is a sorry sight.
32   LADY MACBETH:  A foolish thought, to say a sorry sight.
33   MACBETH:  There's one did laugh in's sleep, and one cried,
34           "Murder!"
35           That they did wake each other: I stood and heard them:

```
 1          But they did say their prayers, and addressed them
 2          Again to sleep.
 3   LADY MACBETH:  There are two lodged together.
 4   MACBETH:  One cried "God bless us!" and "Amen" the
 5          other,
 6          As they had seen me with these hangman's hands:
 7          List'ning their fear, I could not say "Amen",
 8          When they did say "God bless us."
 9   LADY MACBETH:  Consider it not so deeply.
10   MACBETH:  But wherefore could not I pronounce "Amen"?
11          I had most need of blessing, and "Amen"
12          Stuck in my throat.
13   LADY MACBETH:  These deeds must not be thought
14          After these ways; so, it will make us mad.
15   MACBETH:  Methought I heard a voice cry "Sleep no more!
16          Macbeth does murder sleep", the innocent sleep,
17          Sleep that knits up the ravelled sleeve of care,
18          The death of each day's life, sore labour's bath,
19          Balm of hurt minds, great Nature's second course,
20          Chief nourisher in life's feast, —
21   LADY MACBETH:  What do you mean?
22   MACBETH:  Still it cried "Sleep no more!" to all the house:
23          "Glamis hath murdered sleep, and therefore Cawdor
24          Shall sleep no more: Macbeth shall sleep no more!"
25   LADY MACBETH:  Who was it that thus cried? Why, worthy
26          thane,
27          You do unbend your noble strength, to think
28          So brainsickly of things. Go get some water,
29          And wash this filthy witness from your hand.
30          Why did you bring these daggers from the place?
31          They must lie there: go carry them, and smear
32          The sleepy grooms with blood.
33   MACBETH:  I'll go no more:
34          I am afraid to think what I have done;
35          Look on't again I dare not.
```

| | |
|---|---|
| 1 | **LADY MACBETH: Infirm of purpose!** |
| 2 | **Give me the daggers: the sleeping and the dead** |
| 3 | **Are but as pictures: 'tis the eye of childhood** |
| 4 | **That fears a painted devil. If he do bleed,** |
| 5 | **I'll gild the faces of the grooms withal,** |
| 6 | **For it must seem their guilt.** *(She exits. Knocking is heard.)* |
| 7 | **MACBETH: Whence is that knocking?** |
| 8 | **How is't with me, when every noise appalls me?** |
| 9 | **What hands are here? ha! they pluck out mine eyes!** |
| 10 | **Will all great Neptune's ocean wash this blood** |
| 11 | **Clean from my hand? No; this my hand will rather** |
| 12 | **The multitudinous seas incarnadine,** |
| 13 | **Making the green one red.** *(LADY MACBETH returns.)* |
| 14 | **LADY MACBETH: My hands are of your colour; but I shame** |
| 15 | **To wear a heart so white.** *(Knocking)* **I hear a knocking** |
| 16 | **At the south entry: retire we to our chamber:** |
| 17 | **A little water clears us of this deed:** |
| 18 | **How easy is it then! Your constancy** |
| 19 | **Hath left you unattended.** *(Knocking)* **Hark! more knocking.** |
| 20 | **Get on your nightgown, lest occasion call us** |
| 21 | **And show us to be watchers: be not lost** |
| 22 | **So poorly in your thoughts.** |
| 23 | **MACBETH: To know my deed, 'twere best not know myself.** |
| 24 | *(Knocking)* |
| 25 | **Wake Duncan with thy knocking! I would thou couldst!** |
| 26 | *(Exit.)* |
| 27 | |
| 28 | |
| 29 | |
| 30 | |
| 31 | |
| 32 | |
| 33 | |
| 34 | |
| 35 | |

# Macbeth
## Act II, Scene 3

**Characters:** Macduff, Lennox, Lady Macbeth, Macbeth

**Supporting Characters:** Porter, Malcolm, Donalbain, Banquo

It is in this scene that the murder of King Duncan is discovered. Briefly, King Duncan is a well-loved king of eleventh-century Scotland, and we know by the preceding scene that he was murdered by his trustworthy general Macbeth.

Macbeth murdered the King because of one thing: ambition. You see, he had risen as high as he could go in the ranks of the army, and he would not wait for Duncan to die, so he and his wife, Lady Macbeth, plotted to kill him. One must note the importance of Lady Macbeth: it was she who convinced an otherwise confused and hesitant Macbeth to commit the murder. (Refer to Act I, Scene 7 and Act II, Scene 2.)

This scene opens with a knocking at the door. (Please keep in mind that Macbeth, only minutes before, had brutally stabbed King Duncan to death. He had drugged two guards with wine, went into the King's chambers, butchered him, and then Lady Macbeth took the bloody daggers and placed them in the hands of the guards, thereby making them appear to be the murderers.) The Porter, drunk from a night of revelry, speaks about being at the gates of Hell, and the imaginary dead sinners he refers to all have parallel flaws within Macbeth. The Porter, like so many other Shakespearean characters, is used for comic relief to interrupt the intensity of the main action. Macduff and Lennox, two Scottish noblemen, are amused by the Porter's witticisms, but are diverted by Macbeth's entry.

It is obvious that Macbeth is disturbed. He is numbed by what he has done, and he can barely join in the conversation with Macduff and Lennox. When Lennox delivers this lengthy oration about how wild the night has been, with "strange screams of death ... some say the earth was feverous and did shake," all Macbeth can do is utter, "'Twas a rough night."

Macduff, exiting to waken King Duncan, quickly returns with the horrible news that Duncan has been murdered in his chamber. As Macduff cries out the horror of the crisis at hand, Macbeth is realizing the gravity of the situation and pronounces a true verdict upon himself. On the surface, he is showing grief for the murdered King, but inwardly he finds himself in a torturous turmoil:

"Had I but died an hour before this chance,
I had lived a blessed time; for, from this instant,
There's nothing serious in mortality.
All is but toys; renown and grace is dead,
The wine of life is drawn, and the mere lees
Is left this vault to brag of." (Page 32 & 33 lines 32-2)

As for himself, Macbeth feels that he did die an hour before – at the exact moment he stabbed the sleeping Duncan to death. From this point on, there is nothing worthwhile for him in life.

Duncan's two sons, Malcolm and Donalbain, enter and receive the news of their father's death. Macbeth manages to kill the two guards to cover up his crime, all the while assuming the air of grief and indignation. Some find it odd that Lady Macbeth faints when he is describing the bloody corpse of Duncan in terms "unmannerly breech'd with gore." After all, she was the one who so coolly and methodically planned the murder.

At the end of the scene, Macbeth, not suspected by any, agrees to join the others to "stand ... against the undivulg'd pretense ... of treasonous malice."

1   *SETTING:* The courtyard of MACBETH's castle.
2   *AT RISE:* Knocking within. Enter a PORTER.
3
4   **PORTER: Here's a knocking indeed! If a man were porter of**
5     **hell-gate, he should have old turning the key.** *(Knocking)*
6     **Knock, knock, knock! Who's there, i'th' name of Beelzebub?**
7     **Here's a farmer, that hanged himself on th'expectation of**
8     **plenty: come in, time-server; have napkins enow about you;**
9     **here you'll sweat for't.** *(Knocking)* **Knock, knock! Who's**
10     **there, in th'other devil's name? Faith, here's an equivocator,**
11     **that could swear in both the scales against either scale, who**
12     **committed treason enough for God's sake, yet could not**
13     **equivocate to heaven: O, come in, equivocator.** *(Knocking)*
14     **Knock, knock, knock! Who's there? Faith, here's an English**
15     **tailor come hither, for stealing out of a French hose: come in,**
16     **tailor, here you may roast your goose.** *(Knocking)* **Knock,**
17     **knock! never at quiet! What are you? But this place is too**
18     **cold for hell. I'll devil-porter it no further: I had thought to**
19     **have let in some of all professions, that go the primrose**
20     **way to th'everlasting bonfire.** *(Knocking)* **Anon, anon! I**
21     **pray you, remember the porter.** *(Opens the gate. Enter*
22     *MACDUFF and LENNOX.)*
23   **MACDUFF: Was it so late, friend, ere you went to bed,**
24     **That you do lie so late?**
25   **PORTER: Faith, sir, we were carousing till the second cock:**
26     **and drink, sir, is a great provoker of three things.**
27   **MACDUFF: What three things does drink especially provoke?**
28   **PORTER: Marry, sir, nose-painting, sleep, and urine. Lechery,**
29     **sir, it provokes and unprovokes: it provokes the desire,**
30     **but it takes away the performance. Therefore, much drink**
31     **may be said to be an equivocator with lechery: it makes him,**
32     **and it mars him; it sets him on, and it takes him off; it per-**
33     **suades him, and disheartens him; makes him stand to, and**
34     **not stand to: in conclusion, equivocates him in a sleep, and**
35     **giving him the lie, leaves him.**

1   MACDUFF:  I believe drink gave thee the lie last night.
2   PORTER: That it did, sir, i'the very throat on me: but I requited
3       him for his lie, and, I think, being too strong for him, though
4       he took up my legs sometime, yet I made a shift to cast him.
5   MACDUFF:  Is thy master stirring? *(Enter MACBETH.)*
6       Our knocking has awaked him; here he comes.
7   LENNOX:  Good-morrow, noble sir.
8   MACBETH:  Good-morrow, both.
9   MACDUFF:  Is the king stirring, worthy thane?
10  MACBETH:  Not yet.
11  MACDUFF:  He did command me to call timely on him;
12      I have almost slipped the hour.
13  MACBETH:  I'll bring you to him.
14  MACDUFF:  I know this is a joyful trouble to you;
15      But yet 'tis one.
16  MACBETH:  The labour we delight in physics pain.
17      This is the door.
18  MACDUFF:  I'll make so bold to call,
19      For 'tis my limited service. *(Exit.)*
20  LENNOX:  Goes the king hence today?
21  MACBETH:  He does: he did appoint so.
22  LENNOX:  The night has been unruly: where we lay,
23      Our chimneys were blown down, and, as they say,
24      Lamentings heard i'th'air, strange screams of death,
25      And prophesying with accents terrible
26      Of dire combustion and confused events
27      New hatched to th' woeful time. The obscure bird
28      Clamoured the livelong night: some say, the earth
29      Was feverous and did shake.
30  MACBETH:  'Twas a rough night.
31  LENNOX:  My young remembrance cannot parallel
32      a fellow to it. *(Enter MACDUFF.)*
33  MACDUFF:  O horror! horror! horror! Tongue, nor heart,
34      Cannot conceive or name thee!
35  MACBETH, LENNOX:  What's the matter?

1     MACDUFF:  Confusion now hath made his masterpiece!
2        Most sacrilegious murder hath broke ope
3        The Lord's anointed temple, and stole thence
4        The life o'th'building.
5     MACBETH:  What is't you say? the life?
6     LENNOX:  Mean you his majesty?
7     MACDUFF:  Approach the chamber, and destroy your sight
8        With a new Gorgon: do not bid me speak;
9        See, and then speak yourselves.
10    *(Exit MACBETH and LENNOX.)* Awake! awake!
11       Ring the alarum bell! Murder and treason!
12       Banquo and Donalbain! Malcolm! awake!
13       Shake off this downy sleep, death's counterfeit,
14       And look upon death itself! up, up and see
15       The great doom's image! Malcolm! Banquo!
16       As from your graves rise up, and walk like sprites,
17       To countenance this horror! Ring the bell. *(Bell rings.)*
18    LADY MACBETH:  *(Enters.)* What's the business,
19       That such hideous trumpet calls to parley
20       The sleepers of the house? speak, speak!
21    MACDUFF:  O, gentle lady,
22       'Tis not for you to hear what I can speak:
23       The repetition, in a woman's ear,
24       Would murder as it fell. *(Enter BANQUO.)*
25       O Banquo! Banquo!
26       Our royal master's murdered!
27    LADY MACBETH:  Woe, alas!
28       What, in our house?
29    BANQUO:  Too cruel, any where.
30       Dear Duff, I prithee, contradict thyself,
31       And say it is not so. *(MACBETH and LENNOX return.)*
32    MACBETH:  Had I but died an hour before this chance,
33       I had lived a blessed time; for from this instant
34       There's nothing serious in mortality
35       All is but toys: renown and grace is dead,

1     The wine of life is drawn, and the mere lees
2     Is left this vault to brag of.
3     *(Enter MALCOLM and DONALBAIN.)*
4   DONALBAIN: What is amiss?
5   MACBETH: You are, and do not know't:
6     The spring, the head, the fountain of your blood
7     Is stopped — the very source of it is stopped.
8   MACDUFF: Your royal father's murdered.
9   MALCOLM: O, by whom?
10  LENNOX: Those of his chamber, as it seemed, had done't:
11    Their hands and faces were all badged with blood,
12    So were their daggers, which unwiped we found
13    Upon their pillows:
14    They stared and were distracted, no man's life
15    Was to be trusted with them.
16  MACBETH: O, yet I do repent me of my fury,
17    That I did kill them.
18  MACDUFF: Wherefore did you so?
19  MACBETH: Who can be wise, amazed, temp'rate and furious,
20    Loyal and neutral, in a moment? no man:
21    Th'expedition of my violent love
22    Outrun the pauser, reason. Here lay Duncan,
23    His silver skin laced with his golden blood,
24    And his gashed stabs looked like a breach in nature
25    For ruin's wasteful entrance: there, the murderers,
26    Steeped in the colours of their trade, their daggers
27    Unmannerly breeched with gore: who could refrain,
28    That had a heart to love, and in that heart
29    Courage to make's love known?
30  LADY MACBETH: *(Seeming to faint)* Help me hence, ho!
31  MACDUFF: Look to the lady.
32  MALCOLM: *(Aside)* Why do we hold our tongues,
33    That most may claim this argument for ours?
34  DONALBAIN: What should be spoken here, where our fate,
35    Hid in an auger-hole, may rush and seize us?

1      **Let's away.**

2      **Our tears are not yet brewed.**

3    **MALCOLM: Nor our strong sorrow**

4      **Upon the foot of motion.**

5    **BANQUO: Look to the lady.**

6      **And when we have our naked frailties hid,**

7      **That suffer in exposure, let us meet,**

8      **And question this most bloody piece of work,**

9      **To know it further. Fears and scruples shake us:**

10      **In the great hand of God I stand, and thence**

11      **Against the undivulged pretence I fight**

12      **Of treasonous malice.**

13    **MACDUFF: And so do I.**

14    **ALL: So all.**

15    **MACBETH: Let's briefly put on manly readiness.**

16      **And meet i'th'hall together.**

17    **ALL: Well contented.**

18      *(Exit all but MALCOLM and DONALBAIN.)*

19    **MALCOLM: What will you do? Let's not consort with them:**

20      **To show an unfelt sorrow is an office**

21      **Which the false man does easy. I'll to England.**

22    **DONALBAIN: To Ireland, I: our separated fortune**

23      **Shall keep us both the safer: where we are**

24      **There's daggers in men's smiles: the near in blood,**

25      **The nearer bloody.**

26    **MALCOLM: This murderous shaft that's shot**

27      **Hath not yet lighted, and our safest way**

28      **Is to avoid the aim. Therefore to horse,**

29      **And let us not be dainty of leave-taking,**

30      **But shift away: there's warrant in that theft**

31      **Which steals itself when there's no mercy left.**

32      *(Exit all.)*

33

34

35

# Macbeth
## Act V, Scene 1

**Characters:** Lady Macbeth, Doctor, Gentlewoman

This scene is mostly composed of Lady Macbeth's memories and recollections of events past. It also shows us the metaphors of opposites that is utilized by Shakespeare.

For example, in the beginning of the play, Lady Macbeth desired darkness ("Come, thick night"), but now she finds it repelling. Her holding of the candle is her feeble attempt to fill the darkness, the void, if you will, with light. Also, in her sleep-like state she makes reference to washing her hands, or cleansing herself (much like a self-baptism) of Duncan's murder:

"What will these hands ne'er be clean? …
Here's the smell of the blood still;
All the perfumes of Arabia will not sweeten this little hand."

Contrast this passage with her earlier statement in Act II, Scene 2, when she cites that "a little water clears us of this deed. How easy it is then!" Or, note how strikingly similar it is to Macbeth's guilt-stricken passage immediately after murdering Duncan: "Will all great Neptune's ocean wash this blood clean from my hand?"

Dramatically, this scene depicts a turning point in the character of Lady Macbeth. Earlier in the play, she is shown to be cold, calculating, and purposeful. (Refer to the description of Lady Macbeth in Act I, Scene 7.) She has convinced her husband to murder the sleeping King Duncan so he, as a result, could now become the ruler. After Macbeth literally butchers Duncan, it is Lady Macbeth who calmly instructs her confused and numb husband to wash his hands of the blood and act like nothing has happened. And it is this same Lady Macbeth who methodically places the bloody daggers in the hands of the two guards who, earlier, she had drugged to sleep with wine, thereby making them the prime suspects.

But here, late in the play, she is exposing herself as a woman confused by what is happening around her. Her physician and waiting-gentlewoman are discussing Lady Macbeth's sleepwalking. While they converse, Lady Macbeth appears carrying a candle. Her eyes are open, and she constantly rubs her hands together as if she is washing them. Unaware of what she is saying, she speaks about Duncan's bloody murder, the slaying of Macduff's wife, and of Banquo's burial.

As she speaks, it becomes evident that the guilt and suffering as a result from her past actions is crumbling her. In a sense, Shakespeare shows us that "the wages of sin" is indeed a living death, and that murder and madness often return to plague the culprit. This notion draws parallels to what Macbeth said earlier:

"... But in these cases
We still have judgment here: that we but teach
Bloody instructions, which being taught return
To plague th'inventor."

Shocked by all the verbal ramblings and confessions made by Lady Macbeth in her sleep-like state, the doctor tells the gentlewoman that only God can help her now. The doctor leaves, vowing not to tell a soul what he has heard.

1   *SETTING:* Dunsinane. A room in the castle.

2   *AT RISE:* Enter a DOCTOR OF PHYSIC, and a WAITING

3      GENTLEWOMAN.

4

5   DOCTOR: I have two nights watched with you, but can per-

6      ceive no truth in your report. When was it she last

7      walked?

8   GENTLEWOMAN: Since his majesty went into the field, I

9      have seen her rise from her bed, throw her nightgown

10     upon her, unlock her closet, take forth paper, fold it,

11     write upon't, read it, afterwards seal it, and again

12     return to bed; yet all this while in a most fast sleep.

13   DOCTOR: A great perturbation in nature, to receive at once

14     the benefit of sleep and do the effects of watching! In

15     this slumbery agitation, besides her walking and other

16     actual performances, what, at any time, have you heard

17     her say?

18   GENTLEWOMAN: That, sir, which I will not report after

19     her.

20   DOCTOR: You may to me, and 'tis most meet you should.

21   GENTLEWOMAN: Neither to you nor any one, having no wit-

22     ness to confirm my speech. *(Enter LADY MACBETH, with a*

23     *taper.)* Lo you, here she comes! This is her very guise, and

24     upon my life fast asleep. Observe her, stand close.

25   DOCTOR: How came she by that light?

26   GENTLEWOMAN: Why, it stood by her: she has light by

27     her continually, 'tis her command.

28   DOCTOR: You see, her eyes are open.

29   GENTLEWOMAN: Ay, but their sense are shut.

30   DOCTOR: What is it she does now? Look, how she rubs her

31     hands.

32   GENTLEWOMAN: It is an accustomed action with her, to

33     seem thus washing her hands: I have known her contin-

34     ue in this a quarter of an hour.

35   LADY MACBETH: Yet here's a spot.

1 DOCTOR: Hark, she speaks! I will set down what comes
2     from her, to satisfy my remembrance the more strongly.
3 LADY MACBETH: Out, damned spot! out, I say! One: two:
4     why, then 'tis time to do't. Hell is murky! Fie, my lord,
5     fie! a soldier, and afeard? What need we fear who knows
6     it, when none can call our power to accompt? Yet who
7     would have thought the old man to have had so much
8     blood in him?
9 DOCTOR: Do you mark that?
10 LADY MACBETH: The Thane of Fife had a wife; where is
11     she now? What, will these hands ne'er be clean? No
12     more o' that, my lord, no more o' that: you mar all with
13     this starting.
14 DOCTOR: Go to, go to; you have known what you should not.
15 GENTLEWOMAN: She has spoke what she should not, I am
16     sure of that: heaven knows what she has known.
17 LADY MACBETH: Here's the smell of the blood still: all the
18     perfumes of Arabia will not sweeten this little hand.
19     Oh! oh! oh!
20 DOCTOR: What a sigh is there! The heart is sorely charged.
21 GENTLEWOMAN: I would not have such a heart in my
22     bosom, for the dignity of the whole body.
23 DOCTOR: Well, well, well —
24 GENTLEWOMAN: Pray God it be, sir.
25 DOCTOR: This disease is beyond my practice: yet I have
26     known those which have walked in their sleep who have
27     died holily in their beds.
28 LADY MACBETH: Wash your hands, put on your night-
29     gown, look not so pale: I tell you yet again, Banquo's
30     buried; he cannot come out on's grave.
31 DOCTOR: Even so?
32 LADY MACBETH: To bed, to bed: there's knocking at the
33     gate: come, come, come, come, give me your hand:
34     what's done, cannot be undone: to bed, to bed, to bed.
35 *(She exits.)*

1   **DOCTOR: Will she go now to bed?**
2   **GENTLEWOMAN: Directly.**
3   **DOCTOR: Foul whisp'rings are abroad: unnatural deeds**
4        **Do breed unnatural troubles: infected minds**
5        **To their deaf pillows will discharge their secrets:**
6        **More needs she the divine than the physician:**
7        **God, God forgive us all! Look after her,**
8        **Remove from her the means of all annoyance,**
9        **And still keep eyes upon her. So, good night:**
10       **My mind she has mated and amazed my sight:**
11       **I think, but dare not speak.**
12   **GENTLEWOMAN: Good night, good doctor.** *(They exit.)*
13
14
15
16
17
18
19
20
21
22
23
24
25
26
27
28
29
30
31
32
33
34
35

# Macbeth
## Act V, Scene 8

**Characters:** Macbeth, Macduff

**Supporting Characters:** Malcolm, Old Siward, Ross

This, being the final scene of the play, involves a violent sword-fight and the death of the main character, Macbeth.

Before playing this scene, however, one must try to understand the character and underlying motives of Macbeth. First of all, he is a brave and courageous man and is one of King Duncan's most highly regarded and respected generals in his army. However, his fault lies in his ambition. After a victory in battle early in the play, Macbeth happens to come across three witches who foretell his future: not only will be become Thane of Cawdor, but, ultimately, "King Hereafter" (Refer to Act I, Scene 3.) He has risen quickly in the ranks of the army and finds himself in the position of high general. The only way he can gain position and prestige is to be the king himself. Rather than wait for fate to hand him the crown, he, along with the prodding and planning of his wife, Lady Macbeth, kill King Duncan. As a result, the king's two sons, Malcolm and Donalbain, vow to find the murderer and avenge his death.

This final scene depicts the confrontation of the two: Macbeth, ambitious yet misled, facing Macduff, a man who, according to Thomas Marc Parrott of Princeton University, represents strength and simplicity of a soul untouched by any dealing with the power of evil.

On the battlefield, Macbeth scoffs at the idea of committing suicide as a means of escaping the fate slowly overtaking him. Macbeth admits that he has been avoiding Macduff. Macduff, vowing to avenge his father's murder, presses onward and ultimately forces Macbeth to fight. The two exit as the fight progresses, and Malcolm and his allies come into the scene.

Macduff emerges victorious, carrying the decapitated head of Macbeth. This bloody and trunkless figure represents not only revenge for his father's death, but the death of King Duncan, and perhaps a symbol of unity for Scotland. When playing this scene, be very careful that the physical action does not overcome the spoken word. Let the dialog between Macbeth and Macduff be angry and violent, but, above all, let it be genuine and true. The swordfight should show not only the death of an ambitious, confused, and arguably, tragic character, but it should ultimately show the justice found by Macduff. Macbeth's death, though not glamorous, can be depicted as not a victorious one, but as a necessary one. We must, however, feel some pity for Macbeth, for as he was ambitious and fell to the cravings of power, he must ultimately pay the penalty. Shakespeare was morally certain of this in this (and many) plays, when he showed, through various means, that murder, madness, and mayhem will come back to plague and haunt the perpetrator.

1   *SETTING:* Dunsinane. In a field before the castle.
2   *AT RISE:* MACBETH enters.
3
4   MACBETH:  Why should I play the Roman fool, and die
5         On mine own sword? whiles I see lives, the gashes
6         Do better upon them. *(Enter MACDUFF.)*
7   MACDUFF:  Turn, hell-hound, turn.
8   MACBETH:  Of all men else I have avoided thee:
9         But get thee back, my soul is too much charged
10        With blood of thine already.
11  MACDUFF:  I have no words:
12        My voice is in my sword, thou bloodier villain
13        Than terms can give thee out! *(They fight.)*
14  MACBETH:  Thou losest labour.
15        As easy mayest thou the intrenchant air
16        With thy keen sword impress as make me bleed:
17        Let fall thy blade on vulnerable crests,
18        I bear a charmed life, which must not yield
19        To one of woman born.
20  MACDUFF:  Despair thy charm,
21        And let the angel whom thou still hast served
22        Tell thee, Macduff was from his mother's womb
23        Untimely ripped.
24  MACBETH:  Accursed be that tongue that tells me so,
25        For it hath cowed my better part of man!
26        And be these juggling fiends no more believed,
27        That palter with us in a double sense,
28        That keep the word of promise to our ear,
29        And break it to our hope. I'll not fight with thee.
30  MACDUFF:  Then yield thee, coward,
31        And live to be the show and gaze o'th' time.
32        We'll have thee, as our rarer monsters are,
33        Painted upon a pole, and underwrit,
34        "Here may you see the tyrant."
35  MACBETH:  I will not yield,

1        To kiss the ground before young Malcolm's feet,
2        And to be baited with the rabble's curse.
3        Though Birnam wood be come to Dunsinane,
4        And thou opposed, being of no woman born,
5        Yet I will try the last. Before my body
6        I throw my warlike shield: lay on, Macduff,
7        And damned be him that first cries "Hold, enough."
8        *(They exit, fighting. Enter, with drum and colors,*
9        *MALCOLM, SIWARD, ROSS, THANES and SOLDIERS.)*
10     MALCOLM: I would the friends we miss were safe arrived.
11     SIWARD: Some must go off: and yet, by these I see,
12     So great a day as this is cheaply bought.
13     MALCOLM: Macduff is missing, and your noble son.
14     ROSS: Your son, my lord, has paid a soldier's debt:
15     He only lived but till he was a man,
16     The which no sooner had his prowess confirmed
17     In the unshrinking station where he fought,
18     But like a man he died.
19     SIWARD: Then he is dead?
20     ROSS: Ay, and brought off the field: your cause of sorrow
21     Must not be measured by his worth, for then
22     It hath no end.
23     SIWARD: Had he his hurts before?
24     ROSS: Ay, on the front.
25     SIWARD: Why, then, God's soldier be he!
26     Had I as many sons as I have hairs,
27     I would not wish them to a fairer death:
28     And so his knell is knolled.
29     MALCOLM: He's worth more sorrow,
30     And that I'll spend for him.
31     SIWARD: He's worth no more.
32     They say he parted well and paid his score:
33     And so God be with him! Here comes newer comfort.
34     MACDUFF: *(Enters with MACBETH's head.)*
35     Hail, king! for so thou art. Behold where stands

1        Th'usurper's cursed head: the time is free:
2        I see thee compassed with thy kingdom's pearl,
3        That speak my salutation in their minds;
4        Whose voice I desire aloud with mine:
5        Hail, king of Scotland!
6  ALL:  Hail, king of Scotland!
7  MALCOLM:  We shall not spend a large expense of time
8        Before we reckon with your several loves,
9        And make us even with you. My thanes and kinsmen,
10       Henceforth be earls, the first that ever Scotland
11       In such an honour named. What's more to do,
12       Which would be planted newly with the time,
13       As calling home our exiled friends abroad
14       That fled the snares of watchful tyranny,
15       Producing forth the cruel ministers
16       Of this dead butcher and his fiend-like queen,
17       Who, as 'tis thought, by self and violent hands
18       Took off her life; this, and what needful else
19       That calls upon us, by the grace of Grace
20       We will perform in measure, time, and place:
21       So thanks to all at once, and to each one,
22       Whom we invite to see us crowned at Scone.
23       *(Exit.)*
24
25
26
27
28
29
30
31
32
33
34
35

# Much Ado About Nothing
## Act III, Scene 1

**Characters:** Hero, Ursula

**Supporting Character:** Beatrice

**Extra:** Margaret

The premise of this all-female scene is simple, and the scene itself is a delightful one.

Beatrice, who is the vocal focus of the play (in other words, she is the one who *talks* the most), is about to be the recipient of a practical joke, some "planted gossip," so to speak. You see, Beatrice suspects that Benedick is in love with her. He, on the other hand, is a witty and confident young man who adamantly says that he will never marry … despite the fact that he grows more and more in love with her every time he sees her. (In the end, by the way, they become the "perfect match.")

Hero, the Governor's beautiful daughter, tells Margaret, her attendant, to bring Beatrice to the orchard. She is supposed to tell her that Hero and Ursula, another attendant, are talking about her; she is to tell her that she overheard them talking, and that if she sneaked into the honeysuckle bower, she could hear what they are saying and not be seen.

The plan works. They spot Beatrice entering the bower. Ursula delightfully says:

"The pleasant'st angling is to see the fish
Cut with her golden oars the silver stream,
And greedily devour the treacherous bait."
(Page 47 lines 32-34)

In other words, they have the bait set … let the fun begin!

They speak in earshot of Beatrice; they praise the virtues of Benedick, and state that Beatrice could not possibly be the right woman for him:

"But Nature never fram'd a woman's heart
Of prouder stuff than that of Beatrice ...
She cannot love,
Nor take no shape nor project of affection,
She is so self-endeared ...
So turns she every man the wrong side out."

Now imagine Beatrice's reaction to this: she must be furious, shocked, and ready to scream at them. She's sort of like a caged wild-cat, but she is unable to utter a single sound.

To make matters worse, Hero then says that she will go and counsel the gentleman Benedick, and try to "counsel him to fight against his passion."

After Hero and Ursula leave, Beatrice emerges from her hide-away, bursting with newborn fire. She comments that she shall no longer be condemned for her pride and scorn, and she vows to capture the love of Benedick, "Taming my wild heart to thy loving hand."

1  **SETTING:** Leonato's orchard.
2  **AT RISE:** Enter HERO and two gentlewomen, MARGARET and
3      URSULA.
4
5  **HERO: Good Margaret, run thee to the parlour;**
6      **There shalt thou find my cousin Beatrice**
7      **Proposing with the Prince and Claudio.**
8      **Whisper her ear and tell her, I and Ursley**
9      **Walk in the orchard and our whole discourse**
10     **Is all of her; say that thou overheard'st us,**
11     **And bid her steal into the pleached bower,**
12     **Where honeysuckles, ripened by the sun,**
13     **Forbid the sun to enter, like favourites**
14     **Made proud by princes, that advance their pride**
15     **Against that power that bred it: there will she hide her,**
16     **To listen our propose. This is thy office;**
17     **Bear thee well in it and leave us alone.**
18 **MARGARET: I'll make her come, I warrant you, presently.**
19     *(She exits.)*
20 **HERO: Now, Ursula, when Beatrice doth come,**
21     **As we do trace this alley up and down,**
22     **Our talk must only be of Benedick.**
23     **When I do name him, let it be thy part**
24     **To praise him more than ever man did merit:**
25     **My talk to thee must be how Benedick**
26     **Is sick in love with Beatrice. Of this matter**
27     **Is little Cupid's crafty arrow made,**
28     **That only wounds by hearsay. Now begin;**
29     *(Enter BEATRICE behind.)*
30     **For look where Beatrice, like a lapwing, runs**
31     **Close by the ground, to hear our conference.**
32 **URSULA: The pleasant'st angling is to see the fish**
33     **Cut with her golden oars the silver stream,**
34     **And greedily devour the treacherous bait:**
35     **So angle we for Beatrice, who even now**

| | |
|---|---|
| 1 | Is couched in the woodbine coverture. |
| 2 | Fear you not my part of the dialogue. |
| 3 | HERO: Then go we near her, that her ear lose nothing |
| 4 | Of the false sweet bait that we lay for it. |
| 5 | *(Approaching the bower)* |
| 6 | No, truly. Ursula, she is too disdainful. |
| 7 | I know her spirits are as coy and wild |
| 8 | As haggards of the rock. |
| 9 | URSULA: But are you sure |
| 10 | That Benedick loves Beatrice so entirely? |
| 11 | HERO: So says the Prince and my new betrothed lord. |
| 12 | URSULA: And did they bid you tell her of it, madam? |
| 13 | HERO: They did entreat me to acquaint her of it; |
| 14 | But I persuaded them, if they lov'd Benedick, |
| 15 | To wish him wrestle with affection, |
| 16 | And never to let Beatrice know of it. |
| 17 | URSULA: Why did you so? Doth not the gentleman |
| 18 | Deserve as full as fortunate a bed |
| 19 | As ever Beatrice shall couch upon? |
| 20 | HERO: O god of love! I know he doth deserve |
| 21 | As much as may be yielded to a man; |
| 22 | But Nature never fram'd a woman's heart |
| 23 | Of prouder stuff than that of Beatrice. |
| 24 | Disdain and scorn ride sparkling in her eyes, |
| 25 | Misprising what they look on, and her wit |
| 26 | Values itself so highly that to her |
| 27 | All matter else seems weak: she cannot love, |
| 28 | Nor take no shape nor project of affection, |
| 29 | She is so self-endeared. |
| 30 | URSULA: Sure, I think so; |
| 31 | And therefore certainly it were not good |
| 32 | She knew his love, lest she'll make sport at it. |
| 33 | HERO: Why, you speak truth. I never yet saw man, |
| 34 | How wise, how noble, young, how rarely featur'd, |
| 35 | But she would spell him backward. If fair-fac'd, |

| | |
|---|---|
| 1 | She would swear the gentleman should be her sister; |
| 2 | If black, why, Nature, drawing of an antic, |
| 3 | Made a foul blot: if tall, a lance ill-headed; |
| 4 | If low, an agate very vilely cut; |
| 5 | If speaking, why, a vane blown with all winds; |
| 6 | If silent, why, a block moved with none. |
| 7 | So turns she every man the wrong side out, |
| 8 | And never gives to truth and virtue that |
| 9 | Which simpleness and merit purchaseth. |
| 10 | URSULA: Sure, sure, such carping is not commendable. |
| 11 | HERO: No; not to be so odd and from all fashions |
| 12 | As Beatrice is, cannot be commendable. |
| 13 | But who dare tell her so? If I should speak, |
| 14 | She would mock me into air; O, she would laugh me |
| 15 | Out of myself, press me to death with wit. |
| 16 | Therefore let Benedick, like cover'd fire, |
| 17 | Consume away in sighs, waste inwardly. |
| 18 | It were a better death than die with mocks. |
| 19 | Which is as bad as die with tickling. |
| 20 | URSULA: Yet tell her of it; hear what she will say. |
| 21 | HERO: No; rather I will go to Benedick |
| 22 | And counsel him to fight against his passion; |
| 23 | And, truly, I'll devise some honest slanders |
| 24 | To stain my cousin with; one doth not know |
| 25 | How much an ill word may empoison liking. |
| 26 | URSULA: O, do not your cousin such a wrong. |
| 27 | She cannot be so much without true judgment — |
| 28 | Having so swift and excellent a wit |
| 29 | As she is priz'd to have — as to refuse |
| 30 | So rare a gentleman as Signior Benedick. |
| 31 | HERO: He is the only man of Italy, |
| 32 | Always excepted my dear Claudio. |
| 33 | URSULA: I pray you, be not angry with me, madam, |
| 34 | Speaking my fancy; Signior Benedick, |
| 35 | For shape, for bearing, argument, and valour, |

1        Goes foremost in report through Italy.

2    HERO:  Indeed, he hath an excellent good name.

3    URSULA:  His excellence did earn it, ere he had it.

4        When are you married, madam?

5    HERO:  Why, every day, tomorrow. Come, go in;

6        I'll show thee some attires, and have thy counsel

7        Which is the best to furnish me tomorrow.

8    URSULA:  *(Aside)* She's limed, I warrant you.

9        We have caught her, madam.

10   HERO:  *(Aside)* If it proves so, then loving goes by haps:

11      Some Cupid kills with arrows, some with traps.

12      *(Exit HERO and URSULA.)*

13   BEATRICE:  *(Coming forward)* What fire is in mine ears?

14        Can this be true?

15      Stand I condemn'd for pride and scorn so much?

16      Contempt, farewell! and maiden pride, adieu!

17      No glory lives behind the back of such.

18      And, Benedick, love on; I will requite thee,

19      Taming my wild heart to thy loving hand.

20      If thou dost love, my kindness shall incite thee

21      To bind our loves up in a holy band;

22      For others say thou dost deserve, and I

23      Believe it better than reportingly. *(She exits.)*

24

25

26

27

28

29

30

31

32

33

34

35

# Much Ado About Nothing
## Act III, Scene 4

**Characters:** Hero, Margaret, Beatrice

**Extra:** Ursula

This all-female scene, is short, simple, yet very fun to play.

It is the morning on the day Hero, the beautiful daughter of the Governor, is to be married. She is preparing herself for the wedding with the help of Margaret, her attendant.

They first talk of her wedding gown, comparing hers to the very fashionable one recently worn by the Duchess of Milan. But then Margaret, ever the meddler and gossip, quickly turns the conversation to sex:

> HERO: God give me joy to wear it! for my heart is exceeding heavy.
> MARGARET: 'Twill be heavier soon by the weight of a man.
> HERO: Fie upon thee! Art not ashamed?

And when Beatrice, the true talker of the play, enters, the puns on sex continue: she (Beatrice) complains of having a cold and cannot smell Hero's perfume:

> BEATRICE: I am stuffed, cousin; I cannot smell.
> MARGARET: A maid, and stuffed! There's goodly catching of cold.

(You see, in Elizabethan times, to be "stuffed" was a naughty way of saying that you're pregnant!)

But there's more to the scene than that … each character is indeed unique and with separate emotion.

Hero, understandably, is a nervous young bride. She is in love with Claudio, and though they have had a somewhat rocky relationship, she is ready to marry him.

51

Beatrice is also in love, but with a man who claims he will never get married. However, the more he sees Beatrice, the deeper and deeper he falls for her. Her beloved, Benedick, has confessed to himself that he loves her, and she has confessed to herself that she loves him; however, neither one has confessed their love to the other, so both are left wondering how the other feels.

And Margaret, the gossip, really is a playful, meddling woman who just loves to find her way into everyone's business. She is harmless, really, but should be played as a gossip who shows, to the best of her ability, concern for those closest to her.

1  *SETTING:* Hero's apartment.
2  *AT RISE:* Enter HERO, MARGARET, and URSULA.
3
4  HERO: Good Ursula, wake my cousin Beatrice, and desire
5    her to rise.
6  URSULA: I will, lady.
7  HERO: And bid her come hither.
8  URSULA: Well. *(She exits.)*
9  MARGARET: Troth, I think your other rebato were better.
10  HERO: No, pray thee, good Meg, I'll wear this.
11  MARGARET: By my troth, 's not so good; and I warrant
12    your cousin will say so.
13  HERO: My cousin's a fool, and thou art another: I'll wear
14    none but this.
15  MARGARET: I like the new tire within excellently, if the
16    hair were a thought browner; and your gown's a most
17    rare fashion, i' faith. I saw the Duchess of Milan's gown
18    that they praise so.
19  HERO: O, that exceeds, they say.
20  MARGARET: By my troth, 's but a nightgown in respect of
21    yours: cloth o' gold, and cuts, and laced with silver, set
22    with pearls, down sleeves, side sleeves, and skirts, round
23    underborne with a bluish tinsel; but for a fine, quaint,
24    graceful, and excellent fashion, yours is worth ten on't.
25  HERO: God give me joy to wear it! for my heart is exceed-
26    ing heavy.
27  MARGARET: It will be heavier soon by the weight of a man.
28  HERO: Fie upon thee! art not ashamed?
29  MARGARET: Of what, lady? Of speaking honourably? Is
30    not marriage honourable in a beggar? Is not your lord
31    honourable without marriage? I think you would have
32    me say, "saving your reverence, a husband:" an bad
33    thinking do not wrest true speaking, I'll offend nobody:
34    is there any harm in "the heavier for a husband"? None,
35    I think, an it be the right husband and the right wife;

1      otherwise 'tis light, and not heavy: ask my Lady Beat-

2      rice else; here she comes. *(Enter Beatrice.)*

3  HERO: Good morrow, coz.

4  BEATRICE: Good morrow, sweet Hero.

5  HERO: Why, how now? Do you speak in sick tune?

6  BEATRICE: I am out of all other tune, methinks.

7  MARGARET: Clap's into "Light o' love"; that goes without

8      a burden: do you sing it, and I'll dance it.

9  BEATRICE: Ye light o' love with your heels! then, if your

10     husband have stables enough, you'll see he shall lack no

11     barns.

12  MARGARET: O illegitimate construction! I scorn that with

13     my heels.

14  BEATRICE: 'Tis almost five o'clock, cousin; 'tis time you

15     were ready. By my troth, I am exceeding ill: heigh-ho!

16  MARGARET: For a hawk, a horse, or a husband?

17  BEATRICE: For the letter that begins them all, H.

18  MARGARET: Well, an you be not turned Turk, there's no

19     more sailing by the star.

20  BEATRICE: What means the fool, trow?

21  MARGARET: Nothing I; but God send every one their

22     heart's desire!

23  HERO: These gloves the count sent me; they are an excellent

24     perfume.

25  BEATRICE: I am stuffed, cousin; I cannot smell.

26  MARGARET: A maid, and stuffed! There's goodly catching

27     of cold.

28  BEATRICE: O God help me! God help me! How long have

29     you professed apprehension?

30  MARGARET: Ever since you left it. Doth not my wit become

31     me rarely?

32  BEATRICE: It is not seen enough, you should wear it in your

33     cap. By my troth, I am sick.

34  MARGARET: Get you some of this distilled Carduus

35     Benedictus, and lay it to your heart: it is the only thing

1       for a qualm.

2  HERO:  There thou prick'st her with a thistle.

3  BEATRICE:  Benedictus! why Benedictus? You have some

4       moral in this Benedictus.

5  MARGARET:  Moral! no, by my troth, I have no moral

6       meaning; I meant, plain holy-thistle. You may think per-

7       chance that I think you are in love: nay, by 'r lady, I am

8       not such a fool to think what I list, nor I list not to think

9       what I can, nor indeed I cannot think, if I would think

10       my heart out of thinking, that you are in love or that you

11       will be in love or that you can be in love. Yet Benedick

12       was such another, and now is he become a man: he

13       swore he would never marry, and yet now, in despite of

14       his heart, he eats his meat without grudging; and how

15       you may be converted I know not, but methinks you

16       look with your eyes as other women do.

17  BEATRICE:  What pace is this that thy tongue keeps?

18  MARGARET:  Not a false gallop. *(Re-enter URSULA.)*

19  URSULA:  Madam, withdraw; the Prince, the Count, Signior

20       Benedick, Don John, and all the gallants of the town, are

21       come to fetch you to church.

22  HERO:  Help to dress me, good coz, good Meg, good Ursula.

23

24

25

26

27

28

29

30

31

32

33

34

35

# A Midsummer Night's Dream
## Act III, Scene 1

**Characters:** Quince, Snug, Bottom, Flute, Snout, Starveling, Robin Goodfellow (Puck), Titania

**Extras:** Peaseblossom, Cobweb, Moth, Mustardseed

It is crucial first to know the setting of *A Midsummer Night's Dream* is in the land of mythical Athens. Earlier in the play, Egeus, a wealthy man in Athens, has placed judgment on his daughter Hermia for falling in love with Lysander, a young man of whom he disapproves. He wanted Hermia to marry Demetrius, and, because she has disobeyed her father and, according to Athenian law, she must marry Demetrius or die. After the others leave, Hermia and Lysander agree to meet in the woods the following night; they then plan to leave the city and go to a place outside the Athenian jurisdiction where they can be married.

This scene takes place that next night in the very woods where they are to meet. A group of common laboring men, led by Peter Quince, a carpenter, are preparing a play to be given at the upcoming wedding feast of Theseus and Hippolyta. The play is entitled "Pyramus and Thisbe," and this night of rehearsal also happens to be Midsummer's Eve, a time of great rejoicing and mischief among the fairies who live in the woods.

First off in this scene, one should remember that the lovely Titania, Queen of the Fairies, is sleeping nearby, unbeknownst to the acting troupe. No sooner has rehearsal begun than Bottom, a weaver by trade and star of the production, interrupts the rehearsal with some concerns about the show — he fears that the ladies in the audience will be frightened when he, playing the part of Pyramus, draws his sword and kills himself. Snout and Starveling agree, and then Bottom has an idea: to write a prologue assuring the audience the Pyramus is really Bottom and that he really doesn't kill himself.

Snout then has a problem: won't the lion in the play frighten the ladies as well? They banter the idea of another prologue, but Bottom comes up with a better idea — let half of Snug's face show through the lion's skin and let Snug himself reassure the ladies that all will be safe.

Quince agrees, but then he raises what is truly a practical question — how are they going to present a sense of moonlight by which Pyramus and Thisbe meet? By looking in an almanac, he realizes that there will be a moon that night, but he wants someone to impersonate moonshine by carrying a thornbush and a lantern as a symbol of the moonlight itself.

Quince also says that since Pyramus and Thisbe talk through a chink in the wall between their two houses, there must be a wall. Bottom sees a solution to this problem: Snout can be the wall with his clothes smeared in plaster, and he can make a chink with his fingers for the lovers to talk through.

Puck, or Robin Goodfellow, enters unseen and plots some mischief. Bottom exits, and while Thisbe is struggling with the lines, Puck transforms Bottom's head into the head of an ass. Bottom re-enters to speak his lines to Thisbe, and when everyone sees his head, they are frightened and vanish. Bottom is the only one left on stage.

Puck, invisible and inaudible to Bottom, goes after the actors, scaring them with different voices. Bottom, completely unaware of his transformation, thinks his fellow actors are playing a trick to scare him. Trying to show that he is not afraid, Bottom starts singing. His singing awakens Titania. Earlier in the play, Puck had put the nectar of a magic flower in the eyes of Titania, and when she wakes up, she sees Bottom (with the head of an ass) as a gentleman and instantly falls in love with him. She appoints four fairies to attend him. Bottom takes it all in stride; he has such a high opinion of himself that he feels worthy and indeed justified in all this attention.

1   *SETTING:* A forest.
2   *AT RISE:* TITANIA sleeps. Enter QUINCE, SNUG, BOTTOM,
3       FLUTE, SNOUT and STARVELING
4
5   **BOTTOM: Are we all met?**
6   **QUINCE: Pat, pat; and here's a marvellous convenient place**
7       **for our rehearsal. This green plot shall be our stage, this**
8       **hawthorn-brake our tiring-house, and we will do it in**
9       **action, as we will do it before the Duke.**
10  **BOTTOM: Peter Quince!**
11  **QUINCE: What sayest thou, bully Bottom?**
12  **BOTTOM: There are things in this comedy of Pyramus and**
13      **Thisbe that will never please. First, Pyramus must draw**
14      **a sword to kill himself; which the ladies cannot abide.**
15      **How answer you that?**
16  **SNOUT: By 'r lakin, a parlous fear.**
17  **STARVELING: I believe we must leave the killing out, when**
18      **all is done.**
19  **BOTTOM: Not a whit; I have a device to make all well. Write**
20      **me a prologue, and let the prologue seem to say, we will**
21      **do no harm with our swords, and that Pyramus is not**
22      **killed indeed; and for the more better assurance, tell**
23      **them that I Pyramus am not Pyramus, but Bottom the**
24      **weaver; this will put them out of fear.**
25  **QUINCE: Well, we will have such a prologue; and it shall be**
26      **written in eight and six.**
27  **BOTTOM: No, make it two more; let it be written in eight**
28      **and eight.**
29  **SNOUT: Will not the ladies be afeard of the lion?**
30  **STARVELING: I fear it, I promise you.**
31  **BOTTOM: Masters, you ought to consider with yourself; to**
32      **bring in, God shield us, a lion among ladies is a most**
33      **dreadful thing: for there is not a more fearful wild fowl**
34      **than your lion living; and we ought to look to't.**
35  **SNOUT: Therefore another prologue must tell he is not a lion.**

| | |
|---|---|
| 1 | BOTTOM: Nay, you must name his name, and half his face |
| 2 | must be seen through the lion's neck; and he himself |
| 3 | must speak through, saying thus, or to the same defect: |
| 4 | "Ladies," or "Fair ladies," "I would wish you" or "I |
| 5 | would request you," or "I would entreat you, not to fear, |
| 6 | not to tremble: my life for yours. If you think I come |
| 7 | hither as a lion, it were pity of my life. No, I am no such |
| 8 | thing; I am a man as other men are"; and there indeed let |
| 9 | him name his name, and tell them plainly he is Snug the |
| 10 | joiner. |
| 11 | QUINCE: Well, it shall be so: but there is two hard things, |
| 12 | that is, to bring the moonlight into a chamber; for, you |
| 13 | know, Pyramus and Thisbe meet by moonlight. |
| 14 | SNOUT: Doth the moon shine that night we play our play? |
| 15 | BOTTOM: A calendar, a calendar; look in the almanac; find |
| 16 | out moonshine, find out moonshine. |
| 17 | QUINCE: Yes, it doth shine that night. |
| 18 | BOTTOM: Why, then may you leave a casement of the great |
| 19 | chamber window, where we play, open, and the moon |
| 20 | may shine in at the casement. |
| 21 | QUINCE: Ay, or else one must come in with a bush of thorns |
| 22 | and a lantern, and say he comes to disfigure or to pre- |
| 23 | sent the person of moonshine. Then there is another |
| 24 | thing; we must have a wall in the great chamber; for |
| 25 | Pyramus and Thisbe, says the story, did talk through the |
| 26 | chink of a wall. |
| 27 | SNOUT: You can never bring in a wall. What say you, Bottom? |
| 28 | BOTTOM: Some man or other must present Wall; and let |
| 29 | him have some plaster, or some loam, or some rough- |
| 30 | cast about him, to signify wall; or let him hold his |
| 31 | fingers thus; and through that cranny shall Pyramus |
| 32 | and Thisbe whisper. |
| 33 | QUINCE: If that may be, then all is well. Come, sit down, |
| 34 | every mother's son, and rehearse your parts. Pyramus, |
| 35 | you begin; when you have spoken your speech, enter |

1     into that brake; and so every one according to his cue.

2     *(Enter PUCK behind.)*

3   PUCK: What hempen home-spuns have we swaggering here,

4     So near the cradle of the fairy queen?

5     What, a play toward? I'll be an auditor;

6     An actor too, perhaps, if I see cause.

7   QUINCE: Speak, Pyramus. Thisbe, stand forth.

8   BOTTOM: Thisbe, the flowers of odious savours sweet.

9   QUINCE: Odours, odours.

10   BOTTOM: Odours savours sweet;

11     So hath thy breath, my dearest Thisbe dear.

12     But hark, a voice! stay thou but here a while,

13     And by and by I will to thee appear. *(He exits.)*

14   PUCK: A stranger Pyramus than e'er played here!

15   FLUTE: Must I speak now?

16   QUINCE: Ay, marry, must you; for you must understand, he

17     goes but to see a noise that he heard, and is to come again.

18   FLUTE: Most radiant Pyramus, most lily-white of hue,

19     Of colour like the red rose on triumphant briar,

20     Most brisky juvenal, and eke most lovely Jew,

21     As truest horse, that yet would never tire.

22     I'll meet thee, Pyramus, at Ninny's tomb.

23   QUINCE: "Ninus' tomb," man! Why, you must not speak

24     that yet; that you answer to Pyramus. You speak all your

25     part at once, cues and all. Pyramus, enter: your cue is

26     past; it is "never tire."

27   FLUTE: O, — As true as truest horse, that yet would never tire.

28   BOTTOM: *(Re-enters, wearing an ass's head.)*

29     If I were fair, Thisbe, I were only thine.

30   QUINCE: O monstrous! O strange! We are haunted; pray,

31     masters, fly! masters, help!

32     *(Exit all but BOTTOM and PUCK.)*

33   PUCK: I'll follow you, I'll lead you about a round,

34     Through bog, through bush, through brake, through

35       briar;

1    Sometime a horse I'll be, sometime a hound,
2    A hog, a headless bear, sometime a fire;
3    And neigh, and bark, and grunt, and roar, and burn,
4    Like horse, hound, hog, bear, fire, at every turn.
5    *(He exits.)*
6    BOTTOM:  Why do they run away? This is a knavery of
7    them to make me afeard.
8    SNOUT:  *(Enters.)* O Bottom, thou art changed! What do I see
9    on thee?
10   BOTTOM:  What do you see? You see an ass-head of your
11   own, do you? *(Exit SNOUT.)*
12   QUINCE:  *(Enters.)* Bless thee Bottom, bless thee! Thou art
13   translated! *(He exits.)*
14   BOTTOM:  I see their knavery: this is to make an ass of me,
15   to fright me, if they could; but I will not stir from this
16   place, do what they can. I will walk up and down here,
17   and I will sing, that they shall hear I am not afraid.
18   *(Sings)*    The ousel cock, so black of hue,
19              With orange-tawny bill,
20              The throstle with his note so true,
21              The wren with little quill —
22   TITANIA:  *(Waking)* What angel wakes me from my flowery
23       bed?
24   BOTTOM:  *(Sings)* The finch, the sparrow, and the lark,
25              The plain-song cuckoo grey;
26              Whose note full many a man doth mark,
27              And dares not answer nay.
28   For indeed, who would set his wit to so foolish a bird?
29   Who would give a bird the lie, though he cry "cuckoo"
30       never so?
31   TITANIA:  I pray thee, gentle mortal, sing again;
32       Mine ear is much enamoured of thy note;
33       So is mine eye enthralled to thy shape;
34       And thy fair virtue's force perforce doth move me
35       On the first view, to say, to swear, I love thee.

1   BOTTOM:   Methinks, mistress, you should have little reason
2        for that: and to say the truth, reason and love keep little
3        company together nowadays. The more the pity that
4        some honest neighbours will not make them friends.
5        Nay, I can gleek upon occasion.
6   TITANIA:   Thou art as wise as thou art beautiful.
7   BOTTOM:   Not so, neither; but if I had wit enough to get out
8        of this wood, I have enough to serve mine own turn.
9   TITANIA:   Out of this wood do not desire to go;
10       Thou shalt remain here, whether thou wilt or no.
11       I am a spirit of no common rate;
12       The summer still doth tend upon my state,
13       And I do love thee; therefore, go with me.
14       I'll give thee fairies to attend on thee;
15       And they shall fetch thee jewels from the deep,
16       And sing, while thou on pressed flowers dost sleep:
17       And I will purge thy mortal grossness so
18       That thou shalt like an airy spirit go.
19       Peaseblossom, Cobweb, Moth, and Mustardseed!
20       *(Enter four fairies: PEASEBLOSSOM, COBWEB, MOTH,*
21       *and MUSTARDSEED.)*
22   PEASEBLOSSOM:   Ready.
23   COBWEB:   And I.
24   MOTH:   And I.
25   MUSTARDSEED:   And I.
26   ALL:   Where shall we go?
27   TITANIA:   Be kind and courteous to this gentleman:
28       Hop in his walks, and gambol in his eyes;
29       Feed him with apricocks and dewberries,
30       With purple grapes, green figs, and mulberries;
31       The honey-bags steal from the humble-bees,
32       And for night-tapers crop their waxen thighs,
33       And light them at the fiery glow-worm's eyes,
34       To have my love to bed, and to arise;
35       And pluck the wings from painted butterflies

1      To fan the moonbeams from his sleeping eyes;

2      Nod to him, elves, and do him courtesies.

3  PEASEBLOSSOM:  Hail, mortal!

4  COBWEB:  Hail!

5  MOTH:  Hail!

6  MUSTARDSEED:  Hail!

7  BOTTOM:  I cry your worship's mercy heartily; I beseech

8      your worship's name?

9  COBWEB: Cobweb.

10  BOTTOM:  I shall desire you of more acquaintance, good

11      Master Cobweb; if I cut my finger, I shall make bold

12      with you. Your name, honest gentleman?

13  PEASEBLOSSOM:  Peaseblossom.

14  BOTTOM:  I pray you, commend me to Mistress Squash,

15      your mother, and to Master Peascod, your father. Good

16      Master Peaseblossom, I shall desire you of more

17      acquaintance too. Your name, I beseech you, sir?

18  MUSTARDSEED:  Mustardseed.

19  BOTTOM:  Good Master Mustardseed, I know your patience

20      well. That same cowardly, giant-like ox-beef hath

21      devoured many a gentleman of your house. I promise you,

22      your kindred hath made my eyes water ere now. I desire

23      you of more acquaintance, good Master Mustardseed.

24  TITANIA:  Come, wait upon him, lead him to my bower.

25      The moon, methinks, looks with a watery eye,

26      And when she weeps, weeps every little flower,

27      Lamenting some enforced chastity.

28      Tie up my love's tongue, bring him silently. *(Exit all.)*

29

30

31

32

33

34

35

# King Lear
## Act I, Scene 1

**Characters:** Kent, King Lear

**Supporting Characters:** Gloucester, Edmund, King Lear's daughters, Goneril, Regan, and Cordelia

**Extras:** Dukes of Albany and Cornwall

The play opens in King Lear's palace. Through the opening dialog of Kent and Gloucester, we find out that King Lear is about to divide his kingdom and has been contemplating the worth and value of his two sons-in-law, the Dukes of Albany and Cornwall. Furthermore, we realize that Gloucester has two sons, one legitimate and the other illegitimate; he loves them both, but, regarding his younger illegitimate son, he says, "I have so often blushed to acknowledge him, that now I am brazed to't."

King Lear then makes an impressive and noble entrance, his presence announced by the sound of a trumpet. He is accompanied by the Dukes of Albany and Cornwall, along with his three daughters Goneril, Regan, and Cordelia. Lear promptly makes clear his purpose of this meeting: because of his advancing age and a personal need to rid himself of "all cares and business," he is going to divide his kingdom into three parts, each part going to a daughter. He will determine how much will go to each daughter after hearing each one's testimony on how much she loves her father and how devoted she is to him.

Goneril speaks first, and she claims that her love and devotion to him is boundless. He is, according to her, "Dearer than eye-sight, space, and liberty." She also states that she loves him:

"As much as child e'er lov'd, or father found;
A love that makes breath poor, and speech unable;
Beyond all manner of so much I love you."
(Page 67 lines 24-26)

64

In response, King Lear grants her bountiful lands "With shadowy forests and with champains rich'd, with plenteous rivers and wide-skirted meads." The second daughter, Regan, then confesses her love for her father. She says that:

"I profess myself an enemy to all other joys
Which the most precious square of sense possesses;
And find I am alone felicitate
In your dear highness' love." (Page 68 lines 3-7)

In response, the King gives her the same amount of land as he did Goneril.

Cordelia, the youngest daughter (who is the only unmarried one), then speaks: when asked what she has to say to be awarded such property, her response is "Nothing, my lord." King Lear, astonished by this reply, asks her to speak again, warning her that she may mar her fortunes. She flatly tells him:

"Unhappy that I am, I cannot heave
My heart into my mouth. I love your majesty
According to my bond; nor more nor less."
(Page 68 lines 23-25)

Furious, Lear then not only takes her share of the kingdom and gives it to the other two sisters, but he then completely rejects her as his daughter.

At this point, the Earl of Kent speaks out boldly, making reference to his love for and loyalty to the King. He tries, in vain, to argue with Lear about his decision, and is subsequently and vehemently declared a banished man.

The dynamics of this scene are indeed intriguing. The King's entrance is bold and noble and full of power. His daughters state their love for him; he, in turn, grants them large shares of the kingdom. Then, when Cordelia states her case, the tables turn rather abruptly. Lear's fiery temper is amplified by Cordelia's subservient, yet honest, manner; furthermore, when anyone tries to reason with the fiery Lear they catch the brunt of his wrath. When playing this scene, make sure that the tone in the beginning is calm, even, and almost poignantly serene; then, upon the statements of Cordelia, the pace must quicken and the tempers must flare.

1    *SETTING:* King Lear's palace.
2    *AT RISE:* Enter KENT, GLOUCESTER, and EDMUND
3
4    **KENT: I thought the king had more affected the Duke of**
5       **Albany than Cornwall.**
6    **GLOUCESTER: It did always seem so to us: but now, in the**
7       **division of the kingdom, it appears not which of the**
8       **dukes he values most; for qualities are so weigh'd that**
9       **curiosity in neither can make choice of either's moiety.**
10   **KENT: Is not this your son, my lord?**
11   **GLOUCESTER: His breeding, sir, hath been at my charge:**
12       **I have so often blush'd to acknowledge him, that now I**
13       **am braz'd to't. Do you smell a fault?**
14   **KENT: I cannot wish the fault undone, the issue of it being**
15       **so proper.**
16   **GLOUCESTER: But I have a son, sir, by order of law, some**
17       **year elder than this, who yet is no dearer in my account;**
18       **though this knave came something saucily into the world**
19       **before he was sent for, yet was his mother fair. Do you**
20       **know this noble gentleman, Edmund?**
21   **EDMUND: No, my lord.**
22   **GLOUCESTER: My lord of Kent. Remember him hereafter**
23       **as my honourable friend.**
24   **EDMUND: My services to your lordship.**
25   **KENT: I must love you, and sue to know you better.**
26   **EDMUND: Sir, I shall study deserving.**
27   **GLOUCESTER: He hath been out nine years, and away he**
28       **shall again. The king is coming.** *(Enter one bearing a*
29       *coronet, KING LEAR, CORNWALL, ALBANY, GONERIL,*
30       *REGAN, CORDELIA, and ATTENDANTS.)*
31   **LEAR: Attend the lords of France and Burgundy, Gloucester.**
32   **GLOUCESTER: I shall, my liege.** *(Exit GLOUCESTER and*
33       *EDMUND.)*
34   **LEAR: Meantime we shall express our darker purpose.**
35       **Give me the map there. Know that we have divided**

| | |
|---|---|
| 1 | In three our kingdom; and 'tis our fast intent |
| 2 | To shake all cares and business from our age, |
| 3 | Conferring them on younger strengths, while we |
| 4 | Unburden'd crawl toward death. Our son of Cornwall, |
| 5 | And you, our no less loving son of Albany, |
| 6 | We have this hour a constant will to publish |
| 7 | Our daughters' several dowers, that future strife |
| 8 | May be prevented now. The princes, France and |
| 9 | Burgundy, |
| 10 | Great rivals in our youngest daughter's love, |
| 11 | Long in our court have made their amorous sojourn, |
| 12 | And here are to be answer'd. Tell me, my daughters, |
| 13 | Since now we will divest us both of rule, |
| 14 | Interest of territory, cares of state, |
| 15 | Which of you shall we say doth love us most? |
| 16 | That we our largest bounty may extend |
| 17 | Where nature doth with merit challenge. Goneril, |
| 18 | Our eldest-born, speak first. |
| 19 | GONERIL: Sir, I love you more than words can wield the |
| 20 | matter; |
| 21 | Dearer than eyesight, space, and liberty; |
| 22 | Beyond what can be valu'd, rich or rare; |
| 23 | No less than life, with grace, health, beauty, honour; |
| 24 | As much as child e'er lov'd, or father found; |
| 25 | A love that makes breath poor, and speech unable; |
| 26 | Beyond all manner of so much I love you. |
| 27 | CORDELIA: *(Aside)* What shall Cordelia do? Love, and be |
| 28 | silent. |
| 29 | LEAR: Of all these bounds, even from this line to this, |
| 30 | With shadowy forests and with champains rich'd, |
| 31 | With plenteous rivers and wide-skirted meads, |
| 32 | We make thee lady. To thine and Albany's issue |
| 33 | Be this perpetual. What says our second daughter, |
| 34 | Our dearest Regan, wife to Cornwall? Speak. |
| 35 | REGAN: I am made of that self metal as my sister, |

| | |
|---|---|
| 1 | And prize me at her worth. In my true heart |
| 2 | I find she names my very deed of love; |
| 3 | Only she comes too short, that I profess |
| 4 | Myself an enemy to all other joys, |
| 5 | Which the most precious square of sense possesses; |
| 6 | And find I am alone felicitate |
| 7 | In your dear highness' love. |
| 8 | CORDELIA: *(Aside)* Then poor Cordelia! |
| 9 | And yet not so; since, I am sure, my love's |
| 10 | More ponderous than my tongue. |
| 11 | LEAR: To thee and thine hereditary ever |
| 12 | Remain this ample third of our fair kingdom, |
| 13 | No less in space, validity, and pleasure, |
| 14 | Than that conferr'd on Goneril. Now, our joy, |
| 15 | Although the last, not least, to whose young love |
| 16 | The vines of France and milk of Burgundy |
| 17 | Strive to be interess'd, what can you say to draw |
| 18 | A third more opulent than your sisters? Speak. |
| 19 | CORDELIA: Nothing, my lord. |
| 20 | LEAR: Nothing! |
| 21 | CORDELIA: Nothing. |
| 22 | LEAR: Nothing will come of nothing; speak again. |
| 23 | CORDELIA: Unhappy that I am, I cannot heave |
| 24 | My heart into my mouth. I love your majesty |
| 25 | According to my bond; nor more nor less. |
| 26 | LEAR: How, how, Cordelia! mend your speech a little, |
| 27 | Lest you may mar your fortunes. |
| 28 | CORDELIA: Good my lord, |
| 29 | You have begot me, bred me, lov'd me; I |
| 30 | Return those duties back as are right fit, |
| 31 | Obey you, love you, and most honour you. |
| 32 | Why have my sisters husbands, if they say |
| 33 | They love you all? Haply, when I shall wed, |
| 34 | That lord whose hand must take my plight shall carry |
| 35 | Half my love with him, half my care and duty. |

| | |
|---|---|
| 1 | Sure, I shall never marry like my sisters, |
| 2 | To love my father all. |
| 3 | LEAR: But goes thy heart with this? |
| 4 | CORDELIA: Ay, my good lord. |
| 5 | LEAR: So young, and so untender? |
| 6 | CORDELIA: So young, my lord, and true. |
| 7 | LEAR: Let it be so; thy truth then be thy dower: |
| 8 | For, by the sacred radiance of the sun, |
| 9 | The mysteries of Hecate and the night, |
| 10 | By all operation of the orbs |
| 11 | From whom we do exist and cease to be, |
| 12 | Here I disclaim all my paternal care, |
| 13 | Propinquity and property of blood, |
| 14 | And as a stranger to my heart and me |
| 15 | Hold thee from this for ever. The barbarous Scythian, |
| 16 | Or he that makes his generation messes |
| 17 | To gorge his appetite, shall to my bosom |
| 18 | Be as well neighbour'd, pitied, and reliev'd, |
| 19 | As thou my sometime daughter. |
| 20 | KENT: Good my liege, — |
| 21 | LEAR: Peace, Kent! |
| 22 | Come not between the dragon and his wrath. |
| 23 | I lov'd her most, and thought to set my rest |
| 24 | On her kind nursery. Hence, and avoid my sight! |
| 25 | So be my grave my peace, as here I give |
| 26 | Her father's heart from her! Call France. Who stirs? |
| 27 | Call Burgundy. Cornwall and Albany, |
| 28 | With my two daughters' dowers digest this third. |
| 29 | Let pride, which she calls plainness, marry her. |
| 30 | I do invest you jointly with my power, |
| 31 | Pre-eminence, and all the large effects |
| 32 | That troop with majesty. Ourself, by monthly course, |
| 33 | With reservation of an hundred knights |
| 34 | By you to be sustain'd, shall our abode |
| 35 | Make with you by due turn. Only we shall retain |

1        The name, and all th'additions to a king;

2        The sway, revenue, execution of the rest,

3        Beloved sons, be yours; which to confirm,

4        This coronet part betwixt you.

5    KENT: Royal Lear, whom I have ever honour'd as my king,

6        Lov'd as my father, as my master follow'd,

7        As my great patron thought on in my prayers, —

8    LEAR: The bow is bent and drawn, make from the shaft.

9    KENT: Let it fall rather, though the fork invade

10      The region of my heart! Be Kent unmannerly,

11      When Lear is mad. What wouldst thou do, old man?

12      Think'st thou that duty shall have dread to speak,

13      When power to flattery bows? To plainness honour's

14         bound,

15      When majesty falls to folly. Reverse thy doom,

16      And in thy best consideration check

17      This hideous rashness. Answer my life my judgment,

18      Thy youngest daughter does not love thee least;

19      Nor are those empty-hearted whose low sound

20      Reverbs no hollowness.

21    LEAR: Kent, on thy life, no more.

22    KENT: My life I never held but as a pawn

23      To wage against thine enemies; nor fear to lose it,

24      Thy safety being the motive.

25    LEAR: Out of my sight!

26    KENT: See better, Lear; and let me still remain

27      The true blank of thine eye.

28    LEAR: Now, by Apollo, —

29    KENT: Now, by Apollo, king,

30      Thou swear'st thy gods in vain.

31    LEAR: O, vassal, miscreant! *(Laying his hand on his sword.)*

32    ALBANY and CORNWALL: Dear sir, forbear.

33    KENT: Do; kill thy physician, and thy fee bestow

34      Upon the foul disease. Revoke thy gift;

35      Or, whilst I can vent clamour from my throat,

1     I'll tell thee thou dost evil.
2   LEAR:  Hear me, recreant!
3       On thine allegiance, hear me!
4       That thou hast sought to make us break our vows,
5       Which we durst never yet, and with strain'd pride
6       To come betwixt our sentence and our power,
7       Which nor our nature nor our place can bear,
8       Our potency made good, take thy reward.
9       Five days we do allot thee, for provision
10      To shield thee from diseases of the world,
11      And, on the sixth, to turn thy hated back
12      Upon our kingdom; if, on the tenth day following,
13      Thy banish'd trunk be found in our dominions,
14      The moment is thy death. Away! by Jupiter,
15      This shall not be revok'd.
16  KENT:  Fare thee well, king! Sith thus thou wilt appear,
17      Freedom lives hence, and banishment is here.
18      *(To CORDELIA)* The gods to their dear shelter take thee,
19          maid,
20      That justly think'st, and hast most rightly said!
21      *(To REGAN and GONERIL)* And your large speeches may
22          your deeds approve,
23      That good effects may spring from words of love.
24      Thus Kent, O princes! bids you all adieu;
25      He'll shape his old course in a country new.
26      *(Exit all.)*
27
28
29
30
31
32
33
34
35

# As You Like It
## Act I, Scene 1

**Characters:** Orlando, Adam, Oliver, Charles

**Extra:** Dennis

According to Thomas Marc Parrott, Professor of English at Princeton University, *As You Like It*,

> "is a play to be enjoyed rather than analyzed, delightful on the stage ... (it) is a joy forever; it is something better than a well-made play. It is a romance of true love, of freedom, and of happiness, set against a background of Robin Hood's greenwood ... he lavished the treasures of his genius on the sparkling prose, the lyric verse, and above all on the creation of the ideal lady of this world of fantasy, the well-beloved Rosalind."

With that in mind, the play opens in the garden of the house of Oliver de Boys. Orlando, his younger brother, is complaining to Adam, an old family servant, about how he has been treated by Oliver. According to their father's will, Oliver was to make sure that Orlando was trained and raised to become a gentleman, just as he has been doing for their brother Jaques. However, Orlando has been kept at home like a peasant and hasn't received the teachings he deserves. Indeed, he states that "the spirit of my father, which I think is within me, begins to mutiny against this servitude."

When Oliver enters, the two brothers argue and Orlando demands the education and treatment due to him, or else he wants the thousand crowns to which he is entitled (according to the father's will). Oliver snobbishly responds to this threat by saying, "I will not long be troubled with you; you shall have some part of your will."

Orlando and Adam exit, and Oliver is joined by Charles, a

professional wrestler. Charles brings with him important news: the old duke has been banished by his younger brother and has gone into exile in the Forest of Arden and has been joined by some of his loyal lords, where they "live like the old Robin Hood of England ... and fleet the time carelessly, as they did in the golden world." He also says that Rosalind, the Duke's daughter, has remained at the court with her closest companion, Celia.

Charles then states that the new Duke has announced a wrestling match for the next day, and that he is to be pitted against the young Orlando. He tells Oliver that he has heard that Orlando plans to come in disguise and "try a fall" with him. He also states that, although he doesn't want to hurt Orlando, he must wrestle him to the best of his ability to protect his personal honor.

Though Oliver assures him that he need not be concerned, he does state that Orlando is dangerous and may resort to trickery or treachery:

> "... he will practice against thee by poison,
> entrap thee by some treacherous device and never
> leave thee till he hath taken thy life by some indirect
> means or other ..." (Page 79 lines 1-4)

When analyzing this scene, one must first look at the scenario being established: there are two pairs of brothers, and, in each case, a brother is wronged, and wronged for the same reason — because he is well-liked and morally good. According to the mores of the Elizabethan era, the first-born male child inherits his father's property. This is the case with Oliver and Orlando; however, it is just the opposite in the case of the Dukes. It is the younger brother who banishes his older brother into the forest, thereby going against the unwritten laws of the time.

It is also interesting to note, along with the obvious symbolism of city versus idyllic country (nature) utilized here, Shakespeare does a clever trick in the character of Oliver. When Oliver first speaks to Charles, he uses the formal pronoun "you"; however, while warning him of Orlando's possible treachery, labeling him as:

> "... the stubbornest young fellow of France ...
> and envious emulator of every man's good parts,
> a secret and villainous contriver against me ..."

he uses the more familiar pronoun, "thou." This may not seem important, but one must never overlook an opportunity to explore the
character.

1  *SETTING:* Orchard of OLIVER's house.
2  *AT RISE:* Enter ORLANDO and ADAM.
3
4  ORLANDO: As I remember, Adam, it was upon this fashion
5      bequeathed me by will, but poor a thousand crowns,
6      and, as thou sayest, charged my brother, on his blessing,
7      to breed me well: and there begins my sadness. My
8      brother Jaques he keeps at school, and report speaks
9      goldenly of his profit: for my part, he keeps me rustical-
10     ly at home, or (to speak more properly) stays me here at
11     home unkept; for call you that keeping for a gentleman
12     of my birth, that differs not from the stalling of an ox?
13     His horses are bred better, for, besides that they are fair
14     with their feeding, they are taught their manage, and to
15     that end riders dearly hired: but I, his brother, gain
16     nothing under him but growth, for the which his animals
17     on his dunghills are as much bound to him as I. Besides
18     this nothing that he so plentifully gives me, the some-
19     thing that nature gave me his countenance seems to take
20     from me: he lets me feed with his hinds, bars me the
21     place of a brother, and, as much as in him lies, mines my
22     gentility with my education. This is it, Adam, that
23     grieves me, and the spirit of my father, which I think is
24     within me, begins to mutiny against this servitude. I will
25     no longer endure it, though yet I know no wise remedy
26     how to avoid it.
27 ADAM: Yonder comes my master, your brother.
28 ORLANDO: Go apart, Adam, and thou shalt hear how he
29     will shake me up.
30 OLIVER: *(Enters.)* Now, sir! what make you here?
31 ORLANDO: Nothing: I am not taught to make any thing.
32 OLIVER: What mar you then, sir?
33 ORLANDO: Marry, sir, I am helping you to mar that which
34     God made, a poor unworthy brother of yours, with idle-
35     ness.

1   OLIVER:  Marry, sir, be better employed, and be naught
2   awhile.
3   ORLANDO:  Shall I keep your hogs, and eat husks with
4   them? What prodigal portion have I spent, that I should
5   come to such penury?
6   OLIVER:  Know you where you are, sir?
7   ORLANDO:  O, sir, very well; here in your orchard.
8   OLIVER:  Know you before whom, sir?
9   ORLANDO:  Ay, better than him I am before knows me. I
10   know you are my eldest brother, and in the gentle condi-
11   tion of blood you should so know me. The courtesy of
12   nations allows you my better, in that you are the first-
13   born, but the same tradition takes not away my blood,
14   were there twenty brothers betwixt us: I have as much of
15   my father in me as you, albeit I confess your coming
16   before me is nearer to his reverence.
17   OLIVER:  What, boy! *(Strikes him.)*
18   ORLANDO:  Come, come, elder brother, you are too young
19   in this.
20   OLIVER:  Wilt thou lay hands on me, villain?
21   ORLANDO:  I am no villain; I am the youngest son of Sir
22   Rowland de Boys; he was my father, and he is thrice a
23   villain that says such a father begot villains. Wert thou
24   not my brother, I would not take this hand from thy
25   throat till this other had pulled out thy tongue for saying
26   so: thou hast railed on thyself.
27   ADAM:  Sweet masters, be patient; for your father's remem-
28   brance, be at accord.
29   OLIVER:  Let me go, I say.
30   ORLANDO:  I will not, till I please: you shall hear me. My
31   father charged you in his will to give me good education:
32   you have trained me like a peasant, obscuring and hid-
33   ing from me all gentlemanlike qualities. The spirit of my
34   father grows strong in me, and I will no longer endure it;
35   therefore allow me such exercises as may become a

1    gentleman, or give me the poor allottery my father left
2    me by testament; with that I will go buy my fortunes.
3  OLIVER:  And what wilt thou do? beg, when that is spent?
4    Well, sir, get you in: I will not long be troubled with you;
5    you shall have some part of your will: I pray you, leave me.
6  ORLANDO:  I will no further offend you than becomes me
7    for my good.
8  OLIVER:  Get you with him, you old dog.
9  ADAM:  Is "old dog" my reward? Most true, I have lost my
10    teeth in your service. God be with my old master! he
11    would not have spoke such a word. *(Exit ORLANDO and*
12    *ADAM.)*
13  OLIVER:  Is it even so? begin you to grow upon me? I will
14    physic your rankness, and yet give no thousand crowns
15    neither. Holla, Dennis!
16  DENNIS:  *(Enters.)* Calls your worship?
17  OLIVER:   Was not Charles, the Duke's wrestler, here to
18    speak with me?
19  DENNIS:  So please you, he is here at the door, and impor-
20    tunes access to you.
21  OLIVER:  Call him in. *(Exit DENNIS.)* 'Twill be a good way;
22    and tomorrow the wrestling is.
23  CHARLES:  *(Enters.)* Good morrow to your worship.
24  OLIVER:  Good Monsieur Charles, what's the new news at
25    the new court?
26  CHARLES:   There's no news at the court, sir, but the old
27    news: that is, the old Duke is banished by his younger
28    brother the new Duke; and three or four loving lords
29    have put themselves into voluntary exile with him,
30    whose lands and revenues enrich the new Duke; there-
31    fore he gives them good leave to wander.
32  OLIVER:  Can you tell if Rosalind, the Duke's daughter, be
33    banished with her father?
34  CHARLES:  O, no; for the Duke's daughter, her cousin, so
35    loves her, being ever from their cradles bred together,

1      that she would have followed her exile, or have died to
2      stay behind her. She is at the court, and no less beloved
3      of her uncle than his own daughter; and never two ladies
4      loved as they do.
5      OLIVER: Where will the old Duke live?
6      CHARLES: They say he is already in the forest of Arden, and
7      a many merry men with him; and there they live like the
8      old Robin Hood of England: they say many young gen-
9      tlemen flock to him every day, and fleet the time
10     carelessly as they did in the golden world.
11     OLIVER: What, you wrestle tomorrow before the new Duke?
12     CHARLES: Marry, do I, sir; and I came to acquaint you
13     with a matter. I am given, sir, secretly to understand that
14     your younger brother, Orlando, hath a disposition to
15     come in disguised against me to try a fall. Tomorrow, sir,
16     I wrestle for my credit, and he that escapes me without
17     some broken limb shall acquit him well: your brother is
18     but young and tender, and for your love I would be loath
19     to foil him, as I must for my own honour if he come in:
20     therefore, out of my love to you, I came hither to
21     acquaint you withal, that either you might stay him from
22     his intendment, or brook such disgrace well as he shall
23     run into, in that it is a thing of his own search, and alto-
24     gether against my will.
25     OLIVER: Charles, I thank thee for thy love to me, which
26     thou shalt find I will most kindly requite. I had myself
27     notice of my brother's purpose herein, and have by
28     underhand means laboured to dissuade him from it: but
29     he is resolute. I'll tell thee, Charles, it is the stubbornest
30     young fellow of France, full of ambition, an envious
31     emulator of every man's good parts, a secret and villain-
32     ous contriver against me his natural brother: therefore
33     use thy discretion; I had as lief thou didst break his neck
34     as his finger. And thou wert best look to't; for if thou
35     dost him any slight disgrace, or if he do not mightily

1      grace himself on thee, he will practice against thee by
2      poison, entrap thee by some treacherous device, and
3      never leave thee till he hath ta'en thy life by some indi-
4      rect means or other; for I assure thee (and almost with
5      tears I speak it) there is not one so young and so villain-
6      ous this day living. I speak but brotherly of him; but
7      should I anatomize him to thee, as he is, I must blush,
8      and weep, and thou must look pale and wonder.
9   CHARLES: I am heartily glad I came hither to you. If he
10     come tomorrow, I'll give him his payment: if ever he go
11     alone again, I'll never wrestle for prize more: and so,
12     God keep your worship!
13   OLIVER: Farewell, good Charles. *(Exit CHARLES.)* Now will
14     I stir this gamester: I hope I shall see an end of him; for
15     my soul (yet I know not why) hates nothing more than
16     he. Yet he's gentle, never schooled, and yet learned, full
17     of noble device, of all sorts enchantingly beloved, and
18     indeed so much in the heart of the world, and especially
19     of my own people, who best know him, that I am alto-
20     gether misprised: but it shall not be so long, this wrestler
21     shall clear all: nothing remains but that I kindle the boy
22     thither, which now I'll go about. *(He exits.)*
23
24
25
26
27
28
29
30
31
32
33
34
35

# As You Like It
## Act I, Scene 3

**Characters:** Celia, Rosalind, Duke Frederick

This scene takes place in a room in the palace of Duke Frederick. We have learned that the Duke has banished his older brother to the forests; to further complicate the circumstance, his daughter, Celia, is cousin and close companion to Rosalind, the daughter of the banished older brother.

The scene opens with the two young ladies discussing not only the banishment, but the major theme of this outstanding play — love. Here Rosalind confesses her love for Orlando to Celia, and she asks her to love him (in other words, to respect and approve of him) as well. The girls' talk of love is interrupted by the Duke's furious entrance. Angrily, he tells Rosalind that she, too, will be banished from the premises within ten days and promises her that "… if thou be'st found … So near our public court as twenty miles … Thou diest for it." (Page 83 lines 9-11)

At this point, too, one must also understand the plight of Orlando. In a parallel situation to the banishment of Rosalind's father, Orlando is suffering from the hand of his brother as well. According to the will of his father, Orlando's older brother, Oliver, must instruct Orlando on the ways of becoming a gentleman or pay him the thousand crowns that is bequeathed in the will. Oliver refuses to do so, and Orlando, in Act I, Scene 1, insists that Oliver provide him with the education and training that he deserves. (Note, too, that Oliver did provide the proper training for his other brother, Jaques.)

Furthermore, the young Duke has scheduled a wrestling tournament for the next day, pitting Charles, a champion wrestler, against Orlando. In the preceding scene, Oliver tells Charles that Orlando is not to be trusted and plans to defeat Charles with trickery (which is not true).

Here, Duke Frederick's truly evil nature is displayed. He banishes Rosalind from the palace simply because she reminds him of her father: "Thou art thy father's daughter, there's enough." Furthermore, he shows absolutely no guilt or remorse when Celia, his own daughter, says that if Rosalind is banned she will go with her as well. The Duke's response? A curt, "You are a fool."

After the Duke's exit, the girls decide to go alone into the Forest of Arden, but *in disguise*. This was a favorite ploy used to entertain Elizabethan audiences: to disguise young ladies as boys. Rosalind chooses to call herself Ganymede, who, according to mythology, was a Trojan youth abducted to Olympus. Celia decides to call herself Aliena.

They decide to take Touchstone, the court clown, with them. This is another common device used by Shakespeare: often, the clown, or fool, would offer the most keen human insight or be the clearest judge of character during the course of the play.

Thus, the stage is set: the two girls, along with Touchstone, will join Rosalind's banished father in the forest. This play is part fantasy, part discovery of love, and Celia's final quote reflects this mood of "liberation:" "Now go we in content ... To liberty, and not to banishment." (Page 86 lines 4 & 5)

1   *SETTING:* A room in the palace.
2   *AT RISE:* Enter CELIA and ROSALIND
3
4   CELIA: Why, cousin! why, Rosalind! Cupid have mercy! not
5       a word?
6   ROSALIND: Not one to throw at a dog.
7   CELIA: No, thy words are too precious to be cast away upon curs;
8       throw some of them at me; come lame me with reasons.
9   ROSALIND: Then there were two cousins laid up, when the
10      one should be lamed with reasons, and the other mad
11      without any.
12  CELIA: But is all this for your father?
13  ROSALIND: No, some of it is for my child's father. O, how
14      full of briers is this working-day world!
15  CELIA: They are but burs, cousin, thrown upon thee in hol-
16      iday foolery; if we walk not in the trodden paths, our
17      very petticoats will catch them.
18  ROSALIND: I could shake them off my coat; these burs are
19      in my heart.
20  CELIA: Hem them away.
21  ROSALIND: I would try if I could cry hem, and have him.
22  CELIA: Come, come, wrestle with thy affections.
23  ROSALIND: O, they take the part of a better wrestler than
24      myself!
25  CELIA: O, a good wish upon you! you will try in time, in
26      despite of a fall. But, turning these jests out of service, let
27      us talk in good earnest: is it possible, on such a sudden,
28      you should fall into so strong a liking with old Sir Row-
29      land's youngest son?
30  ROSALIND: The Duke my father loved his father dearly.
31  CELIA: Doth it therefore ensue that you should love his son
32      dearly? By this kind of chase, I should hate him, for my
33      father hated his father dearly; yet I hate not Orlando.
34  ROSALIND: No, faith, hate him not, for my sake.
35  CELIA: Why should I not? doth he not deserve well?

1  ROSALIND: Let me love him for that, and do you love him
2    because I do. Look, here comes the Duke.
3  CELIA: With his eyes full of anger. *(Enter DUKE FREDERICK,*
4    *with LORDS.)*
5  DUKE: Mistress, dispatch you with your safest haste,
6    And get you from our court.
7  ROSALIND: Me, uncle?
8  DUKE: You, cousin,
9    Within these ten days if that thou be'st found
10    So near our public court as twenty miles,
11    Thou diest for it.
12  ROSALIND: I do beseech your Grace,
13    Let me the knowledge of my fault bear with me:
14    If with myself I hold intelligence,
15    Or have acquaintance with mine own desires,
16    If that I do not dream, or be not frantic, —
17    As I do trust I am not, — then, dear uncle,
18    Never so much as in a thought unborn
19    Did I offend your Highness.
20  DUKE: Thus do all traitors:
21    If their purgation did consist in words,
22    They are as innocent as grace itself:
23    Let it suffice thee that I trust thee not.
24  ROSALIND: Yet your mistrust cannot make me a traitor:
25    Tell me whereon the likelihood depends.
26  DUKE: Thou art thy father's daughter, there's enough.
27  ROSALIND: So was I when your Highness took his dukedom,
28    So was I when your Highness banish'd him:
29    Treason is not inherited, my lord,
30    Or, if we did derive it from our friends,
31    What's that to me? my father was no traitor:
32    Then, good my liege, mistake me not so much
33    To think my poverty is treacherous.
34  CELIA: Dear sovereign, hear me speak.
35  DUKE: Ay, Celia; we stay'd her for your sake,

| | |
|---|---|
| 1 | Else had she with her father rang'd along. |
| 2 | CELIA: I did not then entreat to have her stay, |
| 3 | It was your pleasure, and your own remorse; |
| 4 | I was too young that time to value her, |
| 5 | But now I know her: if she be a traitor, |
| 6 | Why so am I; we still have slept together, |
| 7 | Rose at an instant, learn'd, play'd, ate together, |
| 8 | And wheresoe'er we went, like Juno's swans, |
| 9 | Still we went coupled and inseparable. |
| 10 | DUKE: She is too subtle for thee; and her smoothness, |
| 11 | Her very silence, and her patience, |
| 12 | Speak to the people, and they pity her. |
| 13 | Thou art a fool, she robs thee of thy name, |
| 14 | And thou wilt show more bright, and seem more virtuous, |
| 15 | When she is gone. Then open not thy lips: |
| 16 | Firm and irrevocable is my doom, |
| 17 | Which I have pass'd upon her; she is banish'd. |
| 18 | CELIA: Pronounce that sentence then on me, my liege; |
| 19 | I cannot live out of her company. |
| 20 | DUKE: You are a fool. You, niece, provide yourself; |
| 21 | If you outstay the time, upon mine honour, |
| 22 | And in the greatness of my word, you die. |
| 23 | *(Exit DUKE FREDERICK and LORDS.)* |
| 24 | CELIA: O my poor Rosalind, whither wilt thou go? |
| 25 | Wilt thou change fathers? I will give thee mine. |
| 26 | I charge thee, be not thou more griev'd than I am. |
| 27 | ROSALIND: I have more cause. |
| 28 | CELIA: Thou hast not, cousin; |
| 29 | Prithee, be cheerful: know'st thou not the Duke |
| 30 | Hath banish'd me, his daughter? |
| 31 | ROSALIND: That he hath not. |
| 32 | CELIA: No, hath not? Rosalind lacks then the love |
| 33 | Which teacheth thee that thou and I am one: |
| 34 | Shall we be sunder'd? shall we part, sweet girl? |
| 35 | No, let my father seek another heir: |

| 1 | Therefore devise with me how we may fly, |
| 2 | Whither to go, and what to bear with us, |
| 3 | And do not seek to take your change upon you, |
| 4 | To bear your griefs yourself, and leave me out; |
| 5 | For by this heaven, now at our sorrows pale, |
| 6 | Say what thou canst, I'll go along with thee. |
| 7 | ROSALIND: Why, whither shall we go? |
| 8 | CELIA: To seek my uncle in the forest of Arden. |
| 9 | ROSALIND: Alas, what danger will it be to us, |
| 10 | (Maids as we are) to travel forth so far? |
| 11 | Beauty provoketh thieves sooner than gold. |
| 12 | CELIA: I'll put myself in poor and mean attire, |
| 13 | And with a kind of umber smirch my face; |
| 14 | The like do you: so shall we pass along, |
| 15 | And never stir assailants. |
| 16 | ROSALIND: Were it not better, |
| 17 | Because that I am more than common tall, |
| 18 | That I did suit me all points like a man, |
| 19 | A gallant curtle-axe upon my thigh, |
| 20 | A boar-spear in my hand? and — in my heart |
| 21 | Lie there what hidden woman's fear there will — |
| 22 | We'll have a swashing and a martial outside, |
| 23 | As many other mannish cowards have, |
| 24 | That do outface it with their semblances. |
| 25 | CELIA: What shall I call thee when thou art a man? |
| 26 | ROSALIND: I'll have no worse a name than Jove's own page, |
| 27 | And therefore look you call me Ganymede; |
| 28 | But what will you be call'd? |
| 29 | CELIA: Something that hath a reference to my state: |
| 30 | No longer Celia, but Aliena. |
| 31 | ROSALIND: But, cousin, what if we assay'd to steal |
| 32 | The clownish fool out of your father's court? |
| 33 | Would he not be a comfort to our travel? |
| 34 | CELIA: He'll go along o'er the wide world with me. |
| 35 | Leave me alone to woo him. Let's away, |

1      And get our jewels and our wealth together,
2      Devise the fittest time, and safest way
3      To hide us from pursuit that will be made
4      After my flight. Now go we in content
5      To liberty, and not to banishment. *(They exit.)*
6
7
8
9
10
11
12
13
14
15
16
17
18
19
20
21
22
23
24
25
26
27
28
29
30
31
32
33
34
35

# As You Like It
## Act II, Scene 3

**Characters:** Orlando, Adam

This scene is simple, straightforward, and honest. But in order to fully understand the two characters, one must know what has transpired thus far.

In Act I, the play begins with Orlando confronting his older brother Oliver. According to their father's will, Oliver was to provide him with education and training for becoming a gentleman. Oliver did provide those services to the other brother, Jaques, but has neglected Orlando. When pressed on the issue, Oliver's snobbish response was, "I will not be long trouble with you."

Indeed, this comment reflects his secret plan. Duke Frederick has scheduled a wrestling match for the following day, pitting Charles, a professional wrestler, against Orlando. Meanwhile, Oliver has met with Charles, and though Charles is a favorite to win, he warns him that Orlando plans to win with treachery and trickery. He states:

" … he will practice against thee by poison,
entrap thee by some treacherous device;
and never leave thee till he hath ta'en thy life
by some indirect means or other …"

(Act I, Scene 1, Page 79 lines 1-4)

Charles agrees to give Orlando his due: "If he come tomorrow, I'll give him his payment." Thus, the characters of the evil Oliver and the good Orlando are established. Also, Adam, the family servant, is subject to Oliver's evil ways and sharp tongue. In Scene 1, he insultingly sneers, "Get you with him, you old dog."

This scene opens with Orlando meeting Adam in front of their house. Orlando has defeated Charles in the wrestling match, and Adam tells him that the news of his victory has spread and that Oliver, angered by Orlando's victory, is planning to burn down his sleeping quarters that very night. He also states that if that fails, he will surely try to find another way to kill him: "… if he fail of that, He will have other means to cut you off. …This is no place; this house is but a butchery. Abhor it, fear it, do not enter it." (Page 89 lines 28 & 29, 31 & 32)

Orlando states that he has no way of making a living, and Adam offers him his life's savings of five hundred crowns and begs him to leave; he also begs Orlando to take him along with him as a servant. Orlando praises him for his loyalty and affection. In his final speech, Orlando shows his gratefulness and humility:

> "But, poor old man, thou prun'st a rotten tree,
> That cannot so much as a blossom yield,
> In lieu of all thy pains and husbandry."

(Page 90 lines 32-34)

Simply stated, this is a scene of two honest and good men. They are victims of an evil brother, but their goodness is clearly shown here. It would be advantageous to refer to the synopsis of Act I, Scene 1, so you can understand the conflict of the Fredericks, other brothers with similar struggles.

1   ***SETTING:*** Before Oliver's house.
2   ***AT RISE:*** Enter ORLANDO and ADAM, meeting.
3
4   **ORLANDO: Who's there?**
5   **ADAM: What, my young master? O my gentle master,**
6       **O my sweet master, O you memory**
7       **Of old Sir Rowland! why, what make you here?**
8       **Why are you virtuous? why do people love you?**
9       **And wherefore are you gentle, strong, and valiant?**
10      **Why would you be so fond to overcome**
11      **The bonny priser of the humorous Duke?**
12      **Your praise is come too swiftly home before you.**
13      **Know you not, master, to some kind of men**
14      **Their graces serve them but as enemies?**
15      **No more do yours: your virtues, gentle master,**
16      **Are sanctified and holy traitors to you.**
17      **O, what a world is this, when what is comely**
18      **Envenoms him that bears it!**
19  **ORLANDO: Why, what's the matter?**
20  **ADAM: O unhappy youth,**
21      **Come not within these doors: within this roof**
22      **The enemy of all your graces lives,**
23      **Your brother, no, no brother, yet the son**
24      **(Yet not the son, I will not call him son)**
25      **Of him I was about to call his father,**
26      **Hath heard your praises, and this night he means**
27      **To burn the lodging where you use to lie,**
28      **And you within it: if he fail of that,**
29      **He will have other means to cut you off.**
30      **I overheard him; and his practices;**
31      **This is no place, this house is but a butchery:**
32      **Abhor it, fear it, do not enter it.**
33  **ORLANDO: Why, whither, Adam, wouldst thou have me go?**
34  **ADAM: No matter whither, so you come not here.**
35  **ORLANDO: What, wouldst thou have me go and beg my food?**

| | |
|---|---|
| 1 | Or with a base and boisterous sword enforce |
| 2 | A thievish living on the common road? |
| 3 | This I must do, or know not what to do: |
| 4 | Yet this I will not do, do how I can; |
| 5 | I rather will subject me to the malice |
| 6 | Of a diverted blood, and bloody brother. |
| 7 | ADAM:  But do not so. I have five hundred crowns, |
| 8 | The thrifty hire I sav'd under your father, |
| 9 | Which I did store to be my foster-nurse, |
| 10 | When service should in my old limbs lie lame, |
| 11 | And unregarded age in corners thrown; |
| 12 | Take that, and He that doth the ravens feed, |
| 13 | Yea, providently caters for the sparrow, |
| 14 | Be comfort to my age! Here is the gold, |
| 15 | All this I give you, let me be your servant; |
| 16 | Though I look old, yet I am strong and lusty; |
| 17 | For in my youth I never did apply |
| 18 | Hot and rebellious liquors in my blood. |
| 19 | Nor did not with unbashful forehead woo |
| 20 | The means of weakness and debility; |
| 21 | Therefore my age is as a lusty winter, |
| 22 | Frosty, but kindly: let me go with you, |
| 23 | I'll do the service of a younger man |
| 24 | In all your business and necessities. |
| 25 | ORLANDO:  O good old man, how well in thee appears |
| 26 | The constant service of the antique world, |
| 27 | When service sweat for duty, not for meed! |
| 28 | Thou art not for the fashion of these times, |
| 29 | Where none will sweat, but for promotion, |
| 30 | And having that do choke their service up, |
| 31 | Even with the having; it is not so with thee. |
| 32 | But, poor old man, thou prun'st a rotten tree, |
| 33 | That cannot so much as a blossom yield, |
| 34 | In lieu of all thy pains and husbandry; |
| 35 | But come thy ways, we'll go along together, |

| | |
|---|---|
| 1 | And ere we have thy youthful wages spent, |
| 2 | We'll light upon some settled low content. |
| 3 | ADAM:  Master, go on, and I will follow thee |
| 4 | To the last gasp, with truth and loyalty; |
| 5 | From seventeen years, till now almost fourscore |
| 6 | Here lived I, but now live here no more. |
| 7 | At seventeen years, many their fortunes seek, |
| 8 | But at fourscore, it is too late a week: |
| 9 | Yet fortune cannot recompense me better |
| 10 | Than to die well, and not my master's debtor. *(They exit.)* |
| 11 | |
| 12 | |
| 13 | |
| 14 | |
| 15 | |
| 16 | |
| 17 | |
| 18 | |
| 19 | |
| 20 | |
| 21 | |
| 22 | |
| 23 | |
| 24 | |
| 25 | |
| 26 | |
| 27 | |
| 28 | |
| 29 | |
| 30 | |
| 31 | |
| 32 | |
| 33 | |
| 34 | |
| 35 | |

# As You Like It
## Act III, Scene 4

**Characters:** Rosalind, Celia

**Extra:** Corin

This short, concise scene is an ideal three-minute scene that can be used in a classroom or for an audition piece. However, for a more advanced class or a more in-depth approach to the characters, especially Rosalind, you should combine it with the next scene as well.

Here is what has happened thus far: Duke Frederick has banned his older brother, Duke Senior, to the Forest of Arden. Also, in his anger, he banished the daughter of Duke Senior, Rosalind, as well because "Thou art thy father's daughter, there's enough." (Act I, Scene 3)

To make matters worse, Rosalind's closest companion is her cousin Celia, who is Duke Frederick's daughter. Hating to see Rosalind go, Celia agrees to go with her to the Forest of Arden, *but they both will travel in disguise.* Here Shakespeare utilizes a trick that continually delighted Elizabethan audiences — he would have the girls disguise themselves as boys, and audiences would marvel at the plot twists that would result from this.

There is another sub-plot that must be addressed. Orlando de Boys, a young Englishman who is noble and pure of heart, has recently learned that his older brother, Oliver, is planning to kill him; he leaves home and goes to the Forest of Arden as well. He takes with him the old family servant, Adam, whose constant concern and care of him, along with his sensitivity and noble behavior, makes him an instant favorite with the audience.

Now the stage is set: Rosalind and Celia are in the Forest of Arden dressed like young men. Rosalind goes by the name of Ganymede, and Celia calls herself Aliena. It is imperative to note that

Rosalind, earlier in the play, confessed to Celia her true and undying love for Orlando. Orlando, too, is in love with Rosalind, but has not had the true opportunity to confess it to her; instead, he has been decorating the trees of the forest by hanging love poems on them and carving the name "Rosalind" onto them.

In Act III, Scene 2, the lovers confronted each other, but Orlando did not recognize Rosalind because of her disguise. Through a witty conversation, Orlando confesses to "Ganymede" that he is lovesick and wishes to be cured of his "lunacy." "I am he that is so loveshaked. I pray you, tell me your remedy."

"Ganymede" offers to "cure" Orlando of his lovesickness by simply doing some "role-playing." Orlando must pretend that young Ganymede is the fair Rosalind and Orlando must visit Ganymede's cottage daily to court Ganymede, who will impersonate Rosalind. Ganymede promises Orlando that he will show him just how silly women are.

Now this scene begins. When this scene opens, Rosalind is at the point of tears. She is sitting in the forest with Celia, waiting for Orlando, who has not kept his first appointment for the "love cure." Celia teases her friend about Orlando's unreliability when Rosalind mentions, almost in passing, that she saw her father in the forest, but that he did not recognize her in disguise. It is not that her father isn't important, but she is more concerned about meeting Orlando.

Corin, the shepherd, enters and offers them a bit of diversion — he tells them to watch the "pageant" of love: Silvius courting the scornful Phebe.

1   *SETTING:* The Forest of Arden.
2   *AT RISE:* Enter ROSALIND and CELIA.
3
4   ROSALIND: Never talk to me, I will weep.
5   CELIA: Do, I prithee, but yet have the grace to consider that
6       tears do not become a man.
7   ROSALIND: But have I not cause to weep?
8   CELIA: As good cause as one would desire, therefore weep.
9   ROSALIND: His very hair is of the dissembling color.
10  CELIA: Something browner than Judas's: marry, his kisses
11      are Judas's own children.
12  ROSALIND: I' faith, his hair is of a good color.
13  CELIA: An excellent color: your chestnut was ever the only
14      color.
15  ROSALIND: And his kissing is as full of sanctity as the touch
16      of holy bread.
17  CELIA: He hath bought a pair of cast lips of Diana: a nun of
18      winter's sisterhood kisses not more religiously; the very
19      ice of chastity is in them.
20  ROSALIND: Buy why did he swear he would come this
21      morning, and comes not?
22  CELIA: Nay, certainly, there is no truth in him.
23  ROSALIND: Do you think so?
24  CELIA: Yes, I think he is not a pick-purse, nor a horse-stealer,
25      but for his verity in love, I do think him as concave as a
26      covered goblet, or a worm-eaten nut.
27  ROSALIND: Not true in love?
28  CELIA: Yes, when he is in, but I think he is not in.
29  ROSALIND: You have heard him swear downright he was.
30  CELIA: "Was" is not "is": besides, the oath of a lover is no
31      stronger than the word of a tapster, they are both the con-
32      firmer of false reckonings; he attends here in the forest on
33      the Duke your father.
34  ROSALIND: I met the Duke yesterday, and had much ques-
35      tion with him: he ask'd me of what parentage I was; I

| | |
|---|---|
| 1 | told him, of as good as he, so he laugh'd and let me go. |
| 2 | But what talk we of fathers, when there is such a man as |
| 3 | Orlando? |
| 4 | CELIA:  O, that's a brave man, he writes brave verses, |
| 5 | speaks brave words, swears brave oaths, and breaks |
| 6 | them bravely, quite traverse athwart the heart of his |
| 7 | lover, as a puisny tilter, than spurs his horse but on one |
| 8 | side, breaks his staff like a noble goose: but all's brave |
| 9 | that youth mounts, and folly guides. Who comes here? |
| 10 | CORIN:  *(Enters.)* Mistress and master, you have oft inquir'd |
| 11 | After the shepherd that complain'd of love, |
| 12 | Who you saw sitting by me on the turf, |
| 13 | Praising the proud disdainful shepherdess |
| 14 | That was his mistress. |
| 15 | CELIA:  Well; and what of him? |
| 16 | CORIN:  If you will see a pageant truly play'd |
| 17 | Between the pale complexion of true love |
| 18 | And the red glow of scorn and proud disdain, |
| 19 | Go hence a little, and I shall conduct you |
| 20 | If you will mark it. |
| 21 | ROSALIND:  O, come, let us remove, |
| 22 | The sight of lovers feedeth those in love: |
| 23 | Brings us to this sight, and you shall say |
| 24 | I'll prove a busy actor in their play. *(They exit.)* |
| 25 | |
| 26 | |
| 27 | |
| 28 | |
| 29 | |
| 30 | |
| 31 | |
| 32 | |
| 33 | |
| 34 | |
| 35 | |

# As You Like It
## Act III, Scene 5

**Characters:** Silvius, Phebe, Rosalind

**Extras:** Celia, Corin

This scene, actually, is a continuation of the preceding scene. (Please read the information regarding Act III, Scene 4.) As Rosalind, Celia and Corin secretly watch Silvius try to court Phebe, we hear her scornfully resisting his advances:

"Now I do frown on thee with all my heart,
And if mine eyes can wound, now let them kill thee."

(Page 98 lines 19 & 20)

As you know from the previous scene, Rosalind has disguised herself as a young man and was waiting to meet her true love, Orlando; her ploy was to cure Orlando of his lovesickness, but he failed to show.

She now interrupts Silvius and Phebe and scolds Phebe for her rudeness and unresponsiveness to Silvius's pleadings. Basically, she says that Phebe is fairly ordinary and she should be flattered that Silvius is attempting to win her heart:

"I see no more in you than in the ordinary
Of nature's sale-work …
But, mistress, know yourself, down on your knees,
And thank heaven, fasting, for a good man's love;
For I must tell you friendly in your ear,
Sell when you can; you are not for all markets."

(Page 99 lines 13-14, 28-31)

Phebe, inexplicably, becomes infatuated with Rosalind. (Keep in mind that Rosalind is dressed as a young man going by the name of Ganymede.) This turn of events delighted Elizabethan audiences. It is a hilarious ploy and can be very fun to play; even today this sort of gender-switching is a surefire comical situation.

Phebe is taken by this attractive young "man"; so much so that she admits that she would rather be scolded by him than wooed by Silvius:
> "Sweet youth, I pray you, chide a year together,
> I had rather hear you chide than this man woo."
(Pages 99 & 100 lines 35-1)
However, after Rosalind, Celia, and Corin exit, Phebe comes to her senses and addresses Silvius's pleas. She consents to accept the company of Silvius because he can "talk of love so well." They then go off to write a taunting letter to Ganymede to repay him for his rudeness.

If you are playing the part of Phebe, be most aware of your reactions to Ganymede's speech: you should play it coy, coquettish, and gradually allow the audience to witness the change in your character as you slowly become enamored with this "young man." It is a hilarious scene, and if played well, your audience will love it.

1 *SETTING:* The Forest of Arden.

2 *AT RISE:* Enter SILVIUS and PHEBE.

3

4 SILVIUS: Sweet Phebe, do not scorn me, do not, Phebe;

5  Say that you love me not, but say not so

6  In bitterness; the common executioner,

7  Whose heart the accustom'd sight of death makes hard,

8  Falls not the axe upon the humbled neck

9  But first begs pardon: will you sterner be

10  Than he that dies and lives by bloody drops?

11  *(Enter ROSALIND, CELIA, and CORIN, behind.)*

12 PHEBE: I would not be thy executioner,

13  I fly thee, for I would not injure thee:

14  Thou tell'st me there is murder in mine eye;

15  'Tis pretty, sure, and very probable,

16  That eyes, that are the frail'st, and softest things,

17  Who shut their coward gates on atomies,

18  Should be call'd tyrants, butchers, murderers!

19  Now I do frown on thee with all my heart,

20  And if mine eyes can wound, now let them kill thee:

21  Now counterfeit to swoon, why now fall down,

22  Or if thou canst not, O, for shame, for shame,

23  Lie not, to say mine eyes are murderers!

24  Now show the wound mine eye hath made in thee,

25  Scratch thee but with a pin, and there remains

26  Some scar of it; lean upon a rush,

27  The cicatrice and capable impressure

28  Thy palm some moment keeps; but now mine eyes,

29  Which I have darted at thee, hurt thee not,

30  Nor, I am sure, there is no force in eyes

31  That can do hurt.

32 SILVIUS: O dear Phebe,

33  If ever, — as that ever may be near, —

34  You meet in some fresh cheek the power of fancy,

35  Then shall you know the wounds invisible

| | |
|---|---|
| 1 | That Love's keen arrows make. |
| 2 | PHEBE: But till that time |
| 3 | Come not thou near me: and when that time comes, |
| 4 | Afflict me with thy mocks, pity me not, |
| 5 | As till that time I shall not pity thee. |
| 6 | ROSALIND: And why, I pray you? Who might be your mother, |
| 7 | That you insult, exult, and all at once, |
| 8 | Over the wretched? What though you have no beauty, |
| 9 | As, by my faith, I see no more in you |
| 10 | Than without candle may go dark to bed; |
| 11 | Must you be therefore proud and pitiless? |
| 12 | Why, what means this? Why do you look on me? |
| 13 | I see no more in you than in the ordinary |
| 14 | Of nature's sale-work. 'Od's my little life, |
| 15 | I think she means to tangle my eyes too: |
| 16 | No, faith, proud mistress, hope not after it, |
| 17 | 'Tis not your inky brows, your black silk hair, |
| 18 | Your bugle eyeballs, nor your cheek of cream, |
| 19 | That can entame my spirits to your worship: |
| 20 | You foolish shepherd, wherefore do you follow her |
| 21 | Like foggy south, puffing with wind and rain? |
| 22 | You are a thousand times a properer man |
| 23 | Than she a woman. 'Tis such fools as you |
| 24 | That makes the world full of ill-favour'd children: |
| 25 | 'Tis not her glass, but you, that flatters her, |
| 26 | And out of you she sees herself more proper |
| 27 | Than any of her lineaments can show her: |
| 28 | But, mistress, know yourself, down on your knees, |
| 29 | And thank heaven, fasting, for a good man's love; |
| 30 | For I must tell you friendly in your ear, |
| 31 | Sell when you can, you are not for all markets: |
| 32 | Cry the man mercy, love him, take his offer, |
| 33 | Foul is most foul, being foul to be a scoffer. |
| 34 | So take her to thee, shepherd: fare you well. |
| 35 | PHEBE: Sweet youth, I pray you, chide a year together, |

1   I had rather hear you chide than this man woo.
2   ROSALIND:  He's fall'n in love with your foulness, and she'll
3       fall in love with my anger. If it be so, as fast as she answers
4       thee with frowning looks, I'll sauce her with bitter words.
5       Why look you so upon me?
6   PHEBE:  For no ill will I bear you.
7   ROSALIND:  I pray you do not fall in love with me,
8       For I am falser than vows made in wine:
9       Besides, I like you not: if you will know my house,
10      'Tis at the tuft of olives, here hard by.
11      Will you go, sister? Shepherd, ply her hard.
12      Come sister. Shepherdess, look on him better,
13      And be not proud, though all the world could see,
14      None could be so abus'd in sight as he.
15      Come, to our flock.
16      *(Exit ROSALIND, CELIA, and CORIN.)*
17  PHEBE:  Dead shepherd, now I find thy saw of might,
18      Who ever lov'd, that lov'd not at first sight?
19  SILVIUS:  Sweet Phebe —
20  PHEBE:  Ha; what say'st thou, Silvius?
21  SILVIUS:  Sweet Phebe, pity me.
22  PHEBE:  Why, I am sorry for thee, gentle Silvius.
23  SILVIUS:  Wherever sorrow is, relief would be:
24      If you do sorrow at my grief in love,
25      By giving love, your sorrow, and my grief,
26      Were both extermin'd.
27  PHEBE:  Thou hast my love, is not that neighbourly?
28  SILVIUS:  I would have you.
29  PHEBE:  Why, that were covetousness.
30      Silvius, the time was that I hated thee;
31      And yet it is not that I bear thee love,
32      But since that thou canst talk of love so well,
33      Thy company, which erst was irksome to me,
34      I will endure; and I'll employ thee too:
35      But do not look for further recompense

| | |
|---|---|
| 1 | Than thine own gladness, that thou art employ'd. |
| 2 | SILVIUS: So holy, and so perfect is my love, |
| 3 | And I in such a poverty of grace, |
| 4 | That I shall think it a most plenteous crop |
| 5 | To glean the broken ears after the man |
| 6 | That the main harvest reaps: lose now and then |
| 7 | A scatter'd smile, and that I'll live upon. |
| 8 | PHEBE: Know'st thou the youth that spoke to me erewhile? |
| 9 | SILVIUS: Not very well, but I have met him oft, |
| 10 | And he hath bought the cottage and the bounds |
| 11 | That the old carlot once was master of. |
| 12 | PHEBE: Think not I love him, though I ask for him; |
| 13 | 'Tis but a peevish boy, yet he talks well; |
| 14 | But what care I for words? yet words do well |
| 15 | When he that speaks them pleases those that hear: |
| 16 | It is a pretty youth, not very pretty, |
| 17 | But, sure, he's proud, and yet his pride becomes him; |
| 18 | He'll make a proper man: the best thing in him |
| 19 | Is his complexion: and faster than his tongue |
| 20 | Did make offence, his eye did heal it up: |
| 21 | He is not very tall, yet for his years he's tall: |
| 22 | His leg is but so so, and yet 'tis well: |
| 23 | There was a pretty redness in his lip, |
| 24 | A little riper, and more lusty red |
| 25 | Than that mix'd in his cheek; 'twas just the difference |
| 26 | Betwixt the constant red and mingled damask. |
| 27 | There be some women, Silvius, had they mark'd him |
| 28 | In parcels as I did, would have gone near |
| 29 | To fall in love with him: but, for my part, |
| 30 | I love him not, nor hate him not; and yet |
| 31 | I have more cause to hate him than to love him, |
| 32 | For what had he to do to chide at me? |
| 33 | He said mine eyes were black, and my hair black, |
| 34 | And, now I am remember'd, scorn'd at me: |
| 35 | I marvel why I answer'd not again, |

1        But that's all one: omittance is no quittance:

2        I'll write to him a very taunting letter,

3        And thou shalt bear it, wilt thou, Silvius?

4  SILVIUS:  Phebe, with all my heart.

5  PHEBE:  I'll write it straight;

6        The matter's in my head, and in my heart,

7        I will be bitter with him, and passing short;

8        Go with me, Silvius. *(They exit.)*

9

10

11

12

13

14

15

16

17

18

19

20

21

22

23

24

25

26

27

28

29

30

31

32

33

34

35

# The Taming of the Shrew
## Act I, Scene 2

**Characters:** Petruchio, Grumio, Hortensio, Gremio

Petruchio, a gentleman from Verona, arrives in Padua with his servant Grumio. Petruchio is self-confident, high-spirited, witty, and good-humored. He has come to Padua to seek a wife, or specifically, "to wive and thrive the best I may." In other words, a wife would be good ... a rich wife would be better.

The opening of this scene finds Petruchio and Grumio outside the gate of Hortensio, Petruchio's friend. A humorous quarrel develops over the misunderstanding of the word "knock"; Hortensio answers the disturbance, breaks up the argument, and addresses the two. After discovering Petruchio's purpose, he jestfully offers to introduce him to Katharina, daughter of Baptista (who was a close friend to Petruchio's late father) and local "shrew": Katharina is indeed wealthy, but is also short-tempered and vile tongued.

Petruchio states that if she is wealthy, he can tolerate her temperament. He claims that he cannot sleep until he meets her and he asks Hortensio to accompany him. Hortensio reluctantly agrees, but says he will go along in the disguise of a music teacher for Bianca, Katharina's sister.

Before approaching this scene, one must understand the characters. As mentioned, Petruchio is self-confident, witty, and good-humored; furthermore, it is important to note that he is also quite adventurous. He lives in the country, his father has recently passed away, and he desires to settle down. One can almost perceive that he doesn't want a marriage of mere convenience; otherwise, he would certainly have sought the hand of Bianca, who is even-tempered and just as wealthy.

It is obvious that Katharina's wild temper is indeed an attraction for him. He states that he will marry Katharina even if she is "as foul as was Florentius' love." (This refers to the old fairy tale wherein

Florentius, a knight, marries an old hag in order to learn the answer to a riddle that will save his life. When he marries her, she is transformed into a beautiful young woman.) Petruchio, then, hopes that "Katherine the curst" will be transformed into a loving and obedient wife.

Grumio, too, shares a sharp wit and confident air, but is not quite as clever as his master, Petruchio. He shows a thick head in his misinterpretation of his master's request that he knock at Hortensio's door, but, later in the scene, his clever and quick tongue is shown in his comments with Gremio, one of Bianca's suitors:

Gremio: O this learning, what a thing it is!

Grumio: O this woodcock, what an ass it is!

Understand that this play contains many scenes that are physically hilarious. Not only is the dialog extremely clever, but the argument that opens this scene can be fun to play because of its rough and raucous nature.

1  *SETTING:* Before HORTENSIO's house.
2  *AT RISE:* Enter PETRUCHIO and GRUMIO.
3
4  PETRUCHIO: Verona, for awhile I take my leave,
5      To see my friends in Padua; but, of all
6      My best beloved and approved friend,
7      Hortensio; and I trow this is his house.
8      Here, sirrah Grumio; knock I say.
9  GRUMIO: Knock, sir! whom should I knock? is there any
10      man has rebused your worship?
11  PETRUCHIO: Villain, I say, knock me here soundly.
12  GRUMIO: Knock you here, sir! why, sir, what am I, sir, that
13      I should knock you here, sir?
14  PETRUCHIO: Villain, I say, knock me at this gate;
15      And rap me well, or I'll knock your knave's pate.
16  GRUMIO: My master is grown quarrelsome. I should knock
17      you first,
18      And then I know after who comes by the worst.
19  PETRUCHIO: Will it not be?
20      Faith, sirrah, an you'll not knock, I'll ring it;
21      I'll try how you can sol, fa, and sing it.
22      *(He wrings GRUMIO by the ears.)*
23  GRUMIO: Help, masters, help! my master is mad.
24  PETRUCHIO: Now, knock when I bid you, sirrah villain!
25  HORTENSIO: *(Enters.)* How now! what's the matter? My
26      old friend Grumio! and my good friend Petruchio! How
27      do you all at Verona?
28  PETRUCHIO: Signior Hortensio, come you to part the fray?
29      *Con tutto il cuore ben trovato*, may I say.
30  HORTENSIO: *All nostra casa ben venuto; molto honorato*
31      *signior mio Petruchio.*
32      Rise, Grumio, rise: we will compound this quarrel.
33  GRUMIO: Nay, 'tis no matter, sir, what he 'leges in Latin. If
34      this be not a lawful cause for me to leave his service, look
35      you, sir, he bid me knock him and rap him soundly, sir:

1     well, was it fit for a servant to use his master so; being,

2     perhaps, for aught I see, two-and-thirty, a pip out?

3     Whom would to God, I had well knock'd at first,

4     Then had not Grumio come by the worst.

5     PETRUCHIO:  A senseless villain! Good Hortensio,

6     I bade the rascal knock upon your gate,

7     And could not get him for my heart to do it.

8     GRUMIO:  Knock at the gate! O heavens! Spake you not

9     these words plain, "Sirrah, knock me here, rap me here,

10    knock me well, and knock me soundly"? And come you

11    now with "knocking at the gate"?

12    PETRUCHIO:  Sirrah, be gone, or talk not, I advise you.

13    HORTENSIO:  Petruchio, patience; I am Grumio's pledge.

14    Why, this 's a heavy chance 'twixt him and you,

15    Your ancient, trusty, pleasant servant Grumio.

16    And tell me now, sweet friend, what happy gale

17    Blows you to Padua here from old Verona?

18    PETRUCHIO:  Such wind as scatters young men through

19     the world

20    To seek their fortunes further than at home,

21    Where small experience grows. But in a few,

22    Signior Hortensio, thus it stands with me:

23    Antonio, my father, is deceas'd,

24    And I have thrust myself into this maze,

25    Haply to wive and thrive as best I may.

26    Crowns in my purse I have and goods at home,

27    And so am come abroad to see the world.

28    HORTENSIO:  Petruchio, shall I then come roundly to thee,

29    And wish thee to a shrewd ill-favour'd wife?

30    Thou'dst thank me but a little for my counsel;

31    And yet I'll promise thee she shall be rich,

32    And very rich: but thou'rt too much my friend,

33    And I'll not wish thee to her.

34    PETRUCHIO:  Signior Hortensio, 'twixt such friends as we,

35    Few words suffice; and therefore, if thou know

| | |
|---|---|
| 1 | One rich enough to be Petruchio's wife, |
| 2 | As wealth is burden of my wooing dance, |
| 3 | Be she as foul as was Florentius' love, |
| 4 | As old as Sibyl, and as curst and shrewd |
| 5 | As Socrates' Xanthippe, or a worse, |
| 6 | She moves me not, or not removes, at least, |
| 7 | Affection's edge in me, were she as rough |
| 8 | As are the swelling Adriatic seas: |
| 9 | I come to wive it wealthily in Padua; |
| 10 | If wealthily, then happily in Padua. |
| 11 | GRUMIO:  Nay, look you, sir, he tells you flatly what his |
| 12 | mind is: why, give him gold enough and marry him to a |
| 13 | puppet or an aglet-baby; or an old trot with ne'er a |
| 14 | tooth in her head, though she have as many diseases as |
| 15 | two-and-fifty horses: why, nothing comes amiss, so |
| 16 | money comes withal. |
| 17 | HORTENSIO:  Petruchio, since we are stepp'd thus far in, |
| 18 | I will continue that I broach'd in jest. |
| 19 | I can, Petruchio, help thee to a wife |
| 20 | With wealth enough, and young and beauteous, |
| 21 | Brought up as best becomes a gentlewoman: |
| 22 | Her only fault, — and that is faults enough, — |
| 23 | Is, that she is intolerable curst |
| 24 | And shrewd and forward, so beyond all measure, |
| 25 | That, were my state far worser than it is, |
| 26 | I would not wed her for a mine of gold. |
| 27 | PETRUCHIO:  Hortensio, peace! thou know'st not gold's |
| 28 | effect: |
| 29 | Tell me her father's name, and 'tis enough; |
| 30 | For I will board her, though she chide as loud |
| 31 | As thunder when the clouds in autumn crack. |
| 32 | HORTENSIO:  Her father is Baptista Minola, |
| 33 | An affable and courteous gentleman; |
| 34 | Her name is Katharina Minola, |
| 35 | Renown'd in Padua for her scolding tongue. |

1  PETRUCHIO:  I know her father, though I know not her;
2      And he knew my deceased father well.
3      I will not sleep, Hortensio, till I see her;
4      And therefore let me be thus bold with you,
5      To give you over at this first encounter,
6      Unless you will accompany me thither.
7  GRUMIO:  I pray you, sir, let him go while the humour lasts.
8      O' my word, an she knew him as well as I do, she would
9      think scolding would do little good upon him. She may,
10      perhaps, call him half a score knaves or so: why, that's
11      nothing: an he begin once, he'll rail in his rope-tricks.
12      I'll tell you what, sir, an she stand him but a little, he will
13      throw a figure in her face, and so disfigure her with it
14      that she shall have no more eyes to see withal than a cat.
15      You know him not, sir.
16  HORTENSIO:  Tarry, Petruchio, I must go with thee,
17      For in Baptista's keep my treasure is:
18      He hath the jewel of my life in hold,
19      His youngest daughter, beautiful Bianca,
20      And her withholds from me and other more,
21      Suitors to her and rivals in my love;
22      Supposing it a thing impossible,
23      For those defects I have before rehears'd,
24      That ever Katharina will be woo'd:
25      Therefore this order hath Baptista ta'en,
26      That none shall have access unto Bianca,
27      Till Katharine the curst have got a husband.
28  GRUMIO:  Katharine the curst!
29      A title for a maid of all titles the worst.
30  HORTENSIO:  Now shall my friend Petruchio do me grace,
31      And offer me, disguis'd in sober robes,
32      To old Baptista as a schoolmaster
33      Well seen in music, to instruct Bianca;
34      That so I may, by this device at least
35      Have leave and leisure to make love to her,

| 1 | And unsuspected court her by herself. |
|---|---|
| 2 | GRUMIO: Here's no knavery! See, to beguile the old folks, |
| 3 | how the young folks lay their heads together! |
| 4 | *(Enter GREMIO and LUCENTIO, disguised, with books* |
| 5 | *under his arm.)* |
| 6 | Master, master, look about you: who goes there, ha? |
| 7 | HORTENSIO: Peace, Grumio! 'tis the rival of my love. |
| 8 | Petruchio, stand by awhile. |
| 9 | GRUMIO: A proper stripling, and an amorous! |
| 10 | GREMIO: O! very well; I have perus'd the note. |
| 11 | Hark you, sir; I'll have them very fairly bound: |
| 12 | All books of love, see that at any hand, |
| 13 | And see you read no other lectures to her. |
| 14 | You understand me. Over and beside |
| 15 | Signior Baptista's liberality, |
| 16 | I'll mend it with a largess. Take your papers too, |
| 17 | And let me have them very well perfum'd; |
| 18 | For she is sweeter than perfume itself |
| 19 | To whom they go to. What will you read to her? |
| 20 | LUCENTIO: Whate'er I read to her, I'll plead for you, |
| 21 | As for my patron, stand you so assur'd, |
| 22 | As firmly as yourself were still in place; |
| 23 | Yea, and perhaps with more successful words |
| 24 | Than you, unless you were a scholar, sir. |
| 25 | GREMIO: O! this learning, what a thing it is. |
| 26 | GRUMIO: O! this woodcock, what an ass it is. |
| 27 | PETRUCHIO: Peace, sirrah! |
| 28 | HORTENSIO: Grumio, mum! God save you, Signior Gremio! |
| 29 | GREMIO: And you're well met, Signior Hortensio. |
| 30 | Trow you whither I am going? To Baptista Minola. |
| 31 | I promis'd to inquire carefully |
| 32 | About a schoolmaster for the fair Bianca; |
| 33 | And, by good fortune, I have lighted well |
| 34 | On this young man; for learning and behaviour |
| 35 | Fit for her turn; well read in poetry |

| | |
|---|---|
| 1 | And other books, good ones, I warrant ye. |
| 2 | HORTENSIO: 'Tis well: and I have met a gentleman |
| 3 | Hath promis'd me to help me to another, |
| 4 | A fine musician to instruct our mistress: |
| 5 | So shall I no whit be behind in duty |
| 6 | To fair Bianca, so belov'd of me. |
| 7 | GREMIO: Belov'd of me, and that my deeds shall prove. |
| 8 | GRUMIO: *(Aside)* And that his bags shall prove. |
| 9 | HORTENSIO: Gremio, 'tis now no time to vent our love: |
| 10 | Listen to me, and if you speak me fair, |
| 11 | I'll tell you news indifferent good for either. |
| 12 | Here is a gentleman whom by chance I met, |
| 13 | Upon agreement from us to his liking, |
| 14 | Will undertake to woo curst Katharine; |
| 15 | Yea, and to marry her, if her dowry please. |
| 16 | GREMIO: So said, so done, is well. |
| 17 | Hortensio, have you told him all her faults? |
| 18 | PETRUCHIO: I know she is an irksome, brawling scold. |
| 19 | If that be all, masters, I hear no harm. |
| 20 | GREMIO: No, sayst me so, friend? What countryman? |
| 21 | PETRUCHIO: Born in Verona, old Antonio's son: |
| 22 | My father dead, my fortune lives for me; |
| 23 | And I do hope good days and long to see. |
| 24 | GREMIO: O, sir, such a life, with such a wife, were strange! |
| 25 | But if you have a stomach, to 't i' God's name: |
| 26 | You shall have me assisting you in all. |
| 27 | But will you woo this wildcat? |
| 28 | PETRUCHIO: Will I live? |
| 29 | GRUMIO: Will he woo her? ay, or I'll hang her. |
| 30 | PETRUCHIO: Why came I hither but to that intent? |
| 31 | Think you a little din can daunt mine ears? |
| 32 | Have I not in my time heard lions roar? |
| 33 | Have I not heard the sea, puff'd up with winds, |
| 34 | Rage like an angry boar chafed with sweat? |
| 35 | Have I not heard great ordnance in the field, |

| | |
|---|---|
| 1 | And heaven's artillery thunder in the skies? |
| 2 | Have I not in a pitched battle heard |
| 3 | Loud 'larums, neighing steeds, and trumpets' clang? |
| 4 | And do you tell me of a woman's tongue, |
| 5 | That gives not half so great a blow to hear |
| 6 | As will a chestnut in a farmer's fire? |
| 7 | Tush, tush! fear boys with bugs. |
| 8 | GRUMIO: *(Aside)* For he fears none. |
| 9 | GREMIO: Hortensio, hark: |
| 10 | This gentleman is happily arriv'd, |
| 11 | My mind presumes, for his own good and ours. |
| 12 | HORTENSIO: I promis'd we would be contributors, |
| 13 | And bear his charge of wooing, whatsoe'er. |
| 14 | GREMIO: And so we will, provided that he win her. |
| 15 | GRUMIO: *(Aside)* I would I were as sure of a good dinner. |
| 16 | |
| 17 | |
| 18 | |
| 19 | |
| 20 | |
| 21 | |
| 22 | |
| 23 | |
| 24 | |
| 25 | |
| 26 | |
| 27 | |
| 28 | |
| 29 | |
| 30 | |
| 31 | |
| 32 | |
| 33 | |
| 34 | |
| 35 | |

# The Taming of the Shrew
## Act II, Scene 1

**Characters:** Petruchio, Katharina, Baptista

**Supporting Characters:** Hortensio, Gremio, Tranio, Bianca

    In this scene, Petruchio, a gentleman of Verona, speaks to Baptista about marrying his daughter Katharina. He mentions that Baptista knew his father, and he also finds out about Katharina's dowry, which is one half of Baptista's lands and twenty thousand crowns (to be received after Baptista's death).

    Though Petruchio has never met Katharina, he has already heard of her short temper and vile tongue. But it is this fiery spirit that attracts him: had he simply wanted a wife, he would have asked for the hand of Bianca, Katharina's sister, who is calm and even-tempered. However, Petruchio wants the challenge, the adventure if you will, of transforming this wild woman into his obedient wife. He admits of his confidence and strong will when talking to Baptista about Katharina:

> "I am as peremptory as she proud-minded;
> And where two raging fires meet together
> They do consume the thing that feeds their fury ...
> So I to her, and so she yields to me;
> For I am rough and woo not like a babe."
> (Page 119 lines 6-8, 11-12)

    As he is about to meet Katharina, Hortensio, his friend disguised as a music teacher, enters "with his head broke." He states that while giving Katharina a music lesson, she took the lute and struck him on the head. This delights Petruchio, and he can't wait to meet her:

> "Now, by the world, it is a lusty wench.
> I love her ten times more than e'er I did.
> O! how I long to have some chat with her!"
> (Page 120 lines 1-3)

Hortensio exits, leaving Petruchio alone to prepare for his meeting with Katharina. In his soliloquy, he explains how he plans to mellow her temper with flattery.

Katharina enters, and the fireworks begin. Petruchio responds to her horrible attitude with praise and uses his wit to make his stance with her. "Asses are made to bear, and so are you," she tells him. "Women are made to bear," he quickly responds, "and so are you."

Though he is flattering to her, he will not be moved — he calls her in the beginning "plain Kate, bonny Kate, and Kate the Curst." During the ensuing banter, she slaps him and he wisely does not strike her back. Instead, he gives a stern warning: "I swear I'll cuff you if you strike [me] again." Apparently, this has an effect on Katharina, because she never strikes him again.

What occurs here is a raucous and hilarious argument between two strong-willed people, each with a different motivation: Katharina swears that she'll never be controlled by any man, and Petruchio is determined to "tame the shrew," and make her an obedient wife.

The argument is lively, spirited, very physical, and laced with strong sexual innuendoes:

Kate: If I be waspish, best beware my sting.
Petruchio: My remedy is, then, to pluck it out.
Kate: Ay, if the fool could find it where it lies.
Petruchio: Who knows not where a wasp does wear
   his sting? In his tail.
Kate: In his tongue.
Petruchio: Whose tongue?
Kate: Yours, if you talk of tails, and so farewell.
Petruchio: What! with my tongue in your tail? Nay,
come again.
     (Page 121 lines 25-35)

Another example:

Katharina: … keep you warm.
Petruchio: Marry. So I mean, sweet Katharine, in thy bed.
     (Page 123 lines 16 & 17)

When the others re-enter, Petruchio informs them that he will marry Katharina on the following Sunday. Katharina responds, "I'll

113

see thee hang'd on Sunday first," and Petruchio says that her attitude is all for show and to save face, and that in private she hung about his neck and showered him with kisses.

Baptista gives his blessing for the wedding, and Petruchio departs to make plans for his upcoming nuptials.

1  *SETTING:* Padua. A room in Baptista's house.
2  *AT RISE:* Enter KATHARINA and BIANCA.
3
4  BIANCA:  Good sister, wrong me not, nor wrong yourself,
5       To make a bondmaid and a slave of me;
6       That I disdain: but for these other gawds,
7       Unbind these hands, I'll pull them off myself,
8       Yea, all my raiment, to my petticoat;
9       Or what you will command me will I do,
10      So well I know my duty to my elders.
11  KATHARINA:  Of all thy suitors, here I charge thee, tell
12      Whom thou lov'st best: see thou dissemble not.
13  BIANCA:  Believe me, sister, of all the men alive
14      I never yet beheld that special face
15      Which I could fancy more than any other.
16  KATHARINA:  Minion, thou liest. Is't not Hortensio?
17  BIANCA:  If you affect him, sister, here I swear
18      I'll plead for you myself, but you shall have him.
19  KATHARINA:  O! then, belike, you fancy riches more:
20      You will have Gremio to keep you fair.
21  BIANCA:  Is it for him you do envy me so?
22      Nay, then you jest; and now I well perceive
23      You have but jested with me all this while:
24      I prithee, sister Kate, untie my hands.
25  KATHARINA:  If that be jest, then all the rest was so.
26  *(Strikes her.)*
27  BAPTISTA:  *(Enters.)* Why, how now, dame! whence grows
28      this insolence?
29      Bianca, stand aside. Poor girl! she weeps.
30      Go ply thy needle; meddle not with her.
31      For shame, thou hilding of a devilish spirit,
32      Why dost thou wrong her that did ne'er wrong thee?
33      When did she cross thee with a bitter word?
34  KATHARINA:  Her silence flouts me, and I'll be reveng'd.
35  *(Flies after BIANCA.)*

1　BAPTISTA: What! in my sight? Bianca, get thee in.
2　*(Exit BIANCA.)*
3　KATHARINA: What! will you not suffer me? Nay, now I see
4　　　She is your treasure, she must have a husband;
5　　　I must dance barefoot on her wedding day,
6　　　And, for your love to her, lead apes in hell.
7　　　Talk not to me: I will go sit and weep
8　　　Till I can find occasion of revenge. *(She exits.)*
9　BAPTISTA: Was ever gentleman thus griev'd as I?
10　　　But who comes here?
11　　　*(Enter GREMIO, with LUCENTIO in the habit of a mean*
12　　　*man; PETRUCHIO, with HORTENSIO as a musician; and*
13　　　*TRANIO, with BIONDELLO bearing a lute and books.)*
14　GREMIO: Good morrow, neighbour Baptista.
15　BAPTISTA: Good morrow, neighbour Gremio. God save
16　　　you, gentlemen!
17　PETRUCHIO: And you, good sir. Pray, have you not a daughter
18　　　Call'd Katharina, fair and virtuous?
19　BAPTISTA: I have a daughter, sir, call'd Katharina.
20　GREMIO: You are too blunt; go to it orderly.
21　PETRUCHIO: You wrong me, Signior Gremio: give me leave.
22　　　I am a gentleman of Verona, sir,
23　　　That, hearing of her beauty and her wit,
24　　　Her affability and bashful modesty,
25　　　Her wondrous qualities and mild behaviour,
26　　　Am bold to show myself a forward guest
27　　　Within your house, to make mine eye the witness
28　　　Of that report which I so oft have heard.
29　　　And, for an entrance to my entertainment,
30　　　I do present you with a man of mine,
31　　　*(Presenting HORTENSIO)*
32　　　Cunning in music and the mathematics,
33　　　To instruct her fully in those sciences,
34　　　Whereof I know she is not ignorant.
35　　　Accept of him, or else you do me wrong:

1    His name is Lieio, born in Mantua.
2    BAPTISTA: You're welcome, sir; and he, for your good sake.
3        But for my daughter, Katharine, this I know,
4        She is not for your turn, the more my grief.
5    PETRUCHIO: I see you do not mean to part with her,
6        Or else you like not of my company.
7    BAPTISTA: Mistake me not; I speak but as I find.
8        Whence are you, sir? what may I call your name?
9    PETRUCHIO: Petruchio is my name; Antonio's son;
10       A man well known throughout all Italy.
11   BAPTISTA: I know him well: you are welcome for his sake.
12   GREMIO: Saving your tale, Petruchio, I pray,
13       Let us, that are poor petitioners, speak too.
14       Backare! you are marvellous forward.
15   PETRUCHIO: O, pardon me, Signior Gremio; I would fain
16       be doing.
17   GREMIO: I doubt it not, sir; but you will curse your wooing.
18       Neighbour, this is a gift very grateful, I am sure of it. To
19       express the like kindness, myself, that have been more
20       kindly beholding to you than any, freely give unto you
21       this young scholar, *(Presenting LUCENTIO)* that has been
22       long studying at Rheims; as cunning in Greek, Latin, and
23       other languages, as the other in music and mathematics.
24       His name is Cambio; pray accept his service.
25   BAPTISTA: A thousand thanks, Signior Gremio; welcome,
26       good Cambio. *(To TRANIO)* But, gentle sir, methinks you
27       walk like a stranger: may I be so bold to know the cause
28       of your coming?
29   TRANIO: Pardon me, sir, the boldness is mine own,
30       That, being a stranger in this city here,
31       Do make myself a suitor to your daughter,
32       Unto Bianca, fair and virtuous.
33       Nor is your firm resolve unknown to me,
34       In the preferment of the eldest sister.
35       This liberty is all that I request,

| | |
|---|---|
| 1 | That, upon knowledge of my parentage, |
| 2 | I may have welcome 'mongst the rest that woo, |
| 3 | And free access and favour as the rest: |
| 4 | And, toward the education of your daughters, |
| 5 | I here bestow a simple instrument, |
| 6 | And this small packet of Greek and Latin books: |
| 7 | If you accept them, then their worth is great. |
| 8 | BAPTISTA: Lucentio is your name, of whence, I pray? |
| 9 | TRANIO: Of Pisa, sir; son to Vincentio. |
| 10 | BAPTISTA: A mighty man of Pisa; by report |
| 11 | I know him well: you are very welcome, sir. |
| 12 | *(To HORTENSIO)* Take you the lute, |
| 13 | *(To LUCENTIO)* and you the set of books; |
| 14 | You shall go see your pupils presently. |
| 15 | Holla within! *(Enter a SERVANT.)* |
| 16 | Sirrah, lead these gentlemen |
| 17 | To my two daughters, and then tell them both |
| 18 | These are their tutors: bid them use them well. |
| 19 | *(Exit SERVANT, with HORTENSIO, LUCENTIO, and* |
| 20 | *BIONDELLO.)* |
| 21 | We will go walk a little in the orchard, |
| 22 | And then to dinner. You are passing welcome, |
| 23 | And so I pray you all to think yourselves. |
| 24 | PETRUCHIO: Signior Baptista, my business asketh haste, |
| 25 | And every day I cannot come to woo. |
| 26 | You knew my father well, and in him me, |
| 27 | Left solely heir to all his lands and goods, |
| 28 | Which I have better'd rather than decreas'd: |
| 29 | Then tell me, if I get your daughter's love, |
| 30 | What dowry shall I have with her to wife? |
| 31 | BAPTISTA: After my death the one half of my lands, |
| 32 | And in possession twenty thousand crowns. |
| 33 | PETRUCHIO: And, for that dowry, I'll assure her of |
| 34 | Her widowhood, be it that she survive me, |
| 35 | In all my lands and leases whatsoever. |

| | |
|---|---|
| 1 | Let specialties be therefore drawn between us, |
| 2 | That covenants may be kept on either hand. |
| 3 | BAPTISTA: Ay, when the special thing is well obtain'd, |
| 4 | That is, her love; for that is all in all. |
| 5 | PETRUCHIO: Why, that is nothing; for I tell you, father, |
| 6 | I am as peremptory as she proud-minded; |
| 7 | And where two raging fires meet together |
| 8 | They do consume the thing that feeds their fury: |
| 9 | Though little fire grows great with little wind, |
| 10 | Yet extreme gusts will blow out fire and all; |
| 11 | So I to her, and so she yields to me; |
| 12 | For I am rough and woo not like a babe. |
| 13 | BAPTISTA: Well mayst thou woo, and happy be thy speed! |
| 14 | But be thou arm'd for some unhappy words. |
| 15 | PETRUCHIO: Ay, to the proof; as mountains are for winds, |
| 16 | That shake not, though they blow perpetually. |
| 17 | *(Re-enter HORTENSIO, with his head broken.)* |
| 18 | BAPTISTA: How now, my friend! why dost thou look so pale? |
| 19 | HORTENSIO: For fear, I promise you, if I look pale. |
| 20 | BAPTISTA: What, will my daughter prove a good musician? |
| 21 | HORTENSIO: I think she'll sooner prove a soldier: |
| 22 | Iron may hold with her, but never lutes. |
| 23 | BAPTISTA: Why, then thou canst not break her to the lute? |
| 24 | HORTENSIO: Why, no; for she hath broke the lute to me. |
| 25 | I did but tell her she mistook her frets, |
| 26 | And bow'd her hand to teach her fingering; |
| 27 | When, with a most impatient devilish spirit, |
| 28 | "Frets, call you these?" quoth she; "I'll fume with them"; |
| 29 | And, with that word, she struck me on the head, |
| 30 | And through the instrument my pate made way; |
| 31 | And there I stood amazed for a while, |
| 32 | As on a pillory, looking through the lute; |
| 33 | While she did call me rascal fiddler, |
| 34 | And twangling Jack; with twenty such vile terms |
| 35 | As she had studied to misuse me so. |

1   PETRUCHIO:  Now, by the world, it is a lusty wench!
2       I love her ten times more than e'er I did:
3       O! how I long to have some chat with her!
4   BAPTISTA:  *(To HORTENSIO)* Well, go with me, and be not
5           so discomfited:
6       Proceed in practice with my younger daughter;
7       She's apt to learn, and thankful for good turns.
8       Signior Petruchio, will you go with us,
9       Or shall I send my daughter Kate to you?
10  PETRUCHIO:  I pray you do; I will attend her here,
11      *(Exit BAPTISTA, GREMIO, TRANIO, and HORTENSIO.)*
12      And woo her with some spirit when she comes.
13      Say that she rail; why then I'll tell her plain
14      She sings as sweetly as a nightingale:
15      Say that she frown; I'll say she looks as clear
16      As morning roses newly wash'd with dew:
17      Say she be mute and will not speak a word;
18      Then I'll commend her volubility,
19      And say she uttereth piercing eloquence;
20      If she do bid me pack; I'll give her thanks,
21      As though she bid me stay by her a week:
22      If she deny to wed; I'll crave the day
23      When I shall ask the banns, and when be married.
24      But here she comes; and now, Petruchio, speak.
25      *(Enter KATHARINA.)*
26      Good morrow, Kate; for that's your name, I hear.
27  KATHARINA:  Well have you heard, but something hard of
28          hearing:
29      They call me Katharine that do talk of me.
30  PETRUCHIO:  You lie, in faith; for you are call'd plain Kate,
31      And bonny Kate, and sometimes Kate the curst;
32      But, Kate, the prettiest Kate in Christendom;
33      Kate of Kate-Hall, my super-dainty Kate,
34      For dainties are all cates: and therefore, Kate,
35      Take this of me, Kate of my consolation;

| | |
|---|---|
| 1 | Hearing thy mildness prais'd in every town, |
| 2 | Thy virtues spoke of, and thy beauty sounded, — |
| 3 | Yet not so deeply as to thee belongs, — |
| 4 | Myself am mov'd to woo thee for my wife. |
| 5 | KATHARINA: Mov'd! in good time: let him that mov'd you |
| 6 | hither |
| 7 | Remove you hence. I knew you at the first, |
| 8 | You were a moveable. |
| 9 | PETRUCHIO: Why, what's a moveable? |
| 10 | KATHARINA: A joint-stool. |
| 11 | PETRUCHIO: Thou hast hit it: come, sit on me. |
| 12 | KATHARINA: Asses are made to bear, and so are you. |
| 13 | PETRUCHIO: Women are made to bear, and so are you. |
| 14 | KATHARINA: No such jade as bear you, if me you mean. |
| 15 | PETRUCHIO: Alas! good Kate, I will not burden thee; |
| 16 | For, knowing thee to be but young and light, — |
| 17 | KATHARINA: Too light for such a swain as you to catch. |
| 18 | And yet as heavy as my weight should be. |
| 19 | PETRUCHIO: Should be! should buz! |
| 20 | KATHARINA: Well ta'en, and like a buzzard. |
| 21 | PETRUCHIO: O slow-wing'd turtle! shall a buzzard take thee? |
| 22 | KATHARINA: Ay, for a turtle, as he takes a buzzard. |
| 23 | PETRUCHIO: Come, come, you wasp; i' faith you are too |
| 24 | angry. |
| 25 | KATHARINA: If I be waspish, best beware my sting. |
| 26 | PETRUCHIO: My remedy is, then, to pluck it out. |
| 27 | KATHARINA: Ay, if the fool could find it where it lies. |
| 28 | PETRUCHIO: Who knows not where a wasp does wear |
| 29 | his sting? |
| 30 | In his tail. |
| 31 | KATHARINA: In his tongue. |
| 32 | PETRUCHIO: Whose tongue? |
| 33 | KATHARINA: Yours, if you talk of tails; and so farewell. |
| 34 | PETRUCHIO: What! with my tongue in your tail? nay, |
| 35 | come again. |

1       Good Kate, I am a gentleman.
2    KATHARINA: That I'll try. *(Striking him)*
3    PETRUCHIO: I swear I'll cuff you if you strike again.
4    KATHARINA: So may you lose your arms:
5       If you strike me, you are no gentleman;
6       And if no gentleman, why then no arms.
7    PETRUCHIO: A herald, Kate? O! put me in thy books.
8    KATHARINA: What is your crest? a coxcomb?
9    PETRUCHIO: A combless cock, so Kate will be my hen.
10   KATHARINA: No cock of mine; you crow too like a craven.
11   PETRUCHIO: Nay, come, Kate, come; you must not look so
12      sour.
13   KATHARINA: It is my fashion when I see a crab.
14   PETRUCHIO: Why, here's no crab, and therefore look not
15      sour.
16   KATHARINA: There is, there is.
17   PETRUCHIO: Then show it me.
18   KATHARINA: Had I a glass, I would.
19   PETRUCHIO: What, you mean my face?
20   KATHARINA: Well aim'd of such a young one.
21   PETRUCHIO: Now, by Saint George, I am too young for you.
22   KATHARINA: Yet you are wither'd.
23   PETRUCHIO: 'Tis with cares.
24   KATHARINA: I care not.
25   PETRUCHIO: Nay, hear you, Kate: in sooth, you 'scape not so.
26   KATHARINA: I chafe you, if I tarry: let me go.
27   PETRUCHIO: No, not a whit; I find you passing gentle.
28      'Twas told me you were rough and coy and sullen,
29      And now I find report a very liar;
30      For thou art pleasant, gamesome, passing courteous,
31      But slow in speech, yet sweet as spring-time flowers:
32      Thou canst not frown, thou canst not look askance,
33      Nor bite the lip, as angry wenches will;
34      Nor hast thou pleasure to be cross in talk;
35      But thou with mildness entertain'st thy wooers,

| | |
|---|---|
| 1 | With gentle conference, soft and affable. |
| 2 | Why does the world report that Kate doth limp? |
| 3 | O slanderous world! Kate, like the hazel-twig, |
| 4 | Is straight and slender, and as brown in hue |
| 5 | As hazelnuts, and sweeter than the kernels. |
| 6 | O! let me see thee walk: thou dost not halt. |
| 7 | KATHARINA: Go, fool, and whom thou keep'st command. |
| 8 | PETRUCHIO: Did ever Dian so become a grove |
| 9 | As Kate this chamber with her princely gait? |
| 10 | O! be thou Dian, and let her be Kate, |
| 11 | And then let Kate be chaste, and Dian sportful! |
| 12 | KATHARINA: Where did you study all this goodly speech? |
| 13 | PETRUCHIO: It is extempore, from my mother-wit. |
| 14 | KATHARINA: A witty mother! witless else her son. |
| 15 | PETRUCHIO: Am I not wise? |
| 16 | KATHARINA: Yes; keep you warm. |
| 17 | PETRUCHIO: Marry, so I mean, sweet Katharine, in thy bed: |
| 18 | And therefore, setting all this chat aside, |
| 19 | Thus in plain terms: your father hath consented |
| 20 | That you shall be my wife; your dowry 'greed on; |
| 21 | And will you, nill you, I will marry you. |
| 22 | Now, Kate, I am a husband for your turn; |
| 23 | For, by this light, whereby I see thy beauty, — |
| 24 | Thy beauty that doth make me like thee well, — |
| 25 | Thou must be married to no man but me: |
| 26 | For I am he am born to tame you, Kate; |
| 27 | And bring you from a wild Kate to a Kate |
| 28 | Conformable as other household Kates. |
| 29 | Here comes your father: never make denial; |
| 30 | I must and will have Katharine to my wife. |
| 31 | *(Re-enter BAPTISTA, GREMIO, and TRANIO.)* |
| 32 | BAPTISTA: Now, Signior Petruchio, how speed you with my |
| 33 | daughter? |
| 34 | PETRUCHIO: How but well, sir? how but well? |
| 35 | It were impossible I should speed amiss. |

1 BAPTISTA: Why, how now, daughter Katharine! in your
2     dumps?
3 KATHARINA: Call you me daughter? now, I promise you
4     You have show'd a tender fatherly regard,
5     To wish me wed to one half lunatic;
6     A mad-cap ruffian and a swearing Jack,
7     That thinks with oaths to face the matter out.
8 PETRUCHIO: Father, 'tis thus: yourself and all the world,
9     That talk'd of her, have talk'd amiss of her:
10     If she be curst, it is for policy,
11     For she's not forward, but modest as the dove;
12     She is not hot, but temperate as the morn;
13     For patience she will prove a second Grissel,
14     And Roman Lucrece for her chastity;
15     And to conclude, we have 'greed so well together,
16     That upon Sunday is the wedding day.
17 KATHARINA: I'll see thee hang'd on Sunday first.
18 GREMIO: Hark, Petruchio: she says she'll see thee hang'd
19     first.
20 TRANIO: Is this your speeding? nay then, good night our part!
21 PETRUCHIO: Be patient, gentlemen; I choose her for myself:
22     If she and I be pleas'd, what's that to you?
23     'Tis bargain'd 'twixt us twain, being alone,
24     That she shall still be curst in company.
25     I tell you, 'tis incredible to believe
26     How much she loves me: O! the kindest Kate
27     She hung about my neck, and kiss on kiss
28     She vied so fast, protesting oath on oath,
29     That in a twink she won me to her love.
30     O! you are novices: 'tis a world to see,
31     How tame, when men and women are alone,
32     A meacock wretch can make the curstest shrew.
33     Give me thy hand, Kate: I will unto Venice
34     To buy apparel 'gainst the wedding day.
35     Provide the feast, father, and bid the guests;

| 1 | I will be sure my Katharine shall be fine. |
| 2 | BAPTISTA: I know not what to say; but give me your hands. |
| 3 | God send you joy, Petruchio! 'tis a match. |
| 4 | GREMIO and TRANIO: Amen, say we: we will be witnesses. |
| 5 | PETRUCHIO: Father, and wife, and gentlemen, adieu. |
| 6 | I will to Venice; Sunday comes apace: |
| 7 | We will have rings, and things, and fine array; |
| 8 | And, kiss me, Kate, we will be married o' Sunday. |
| 9 | *(PETRUCHIO and KATHARINA exit.)* |
| 10 | |
| 11 | |
| 12 | |
| 13 | |
| 14 | |
| 15 | |
| 16 | |
| 17 | |
| 18 | |
| 19 | |
| 20 | |
| 21 | |
| 22 | |
| 23 | |
| 24 | |
| 25 | |
| 26 | |
| 27 | |
| 28 | |
| 29 | |
| 30 | |
| 31 | |
| 32 | |
| 33 | |
| 34 | |
| 35 | |

# The Taming of the Shrew
## Act IV, Scene 3

**Characters:** Katharina, Grumio, Petruchio

**Supporting Characters:** Hortensio, Tailor, Haberdasher

In order to fully understand this scene, one must truly understand each character and his/her motivations. Petruchio, a gentleman from Verona, has come to Padua seeking a wife. He is self-confident, witty, and highly adventurous. His friend Hortensio has told him about Katharina, a single woman from a wealthy family, and he also warns him of her hot temper and wild behavior.

This not only intrigues Petruchio, but it excites him as well, for he is a strong-willed man who loves a challenge. For him, this could prove to be his ultimate challenge; for Katharina is no easy task; indeed, had he wanted a calm woman he would have sought the hand of Bianca, her sister (refer to Act II, Scene 1).

At this point in the play, Petruchio has taken Katharina back to his home in Padua and is in the process of "taming" her. This scene opens with Katharina begging Grumio, Petruchio's servant, for some food. Grumio imitates Petruchio's treatment of her by teasing her with suggestions on how to serve some meat. Angrily, she beats Grumio and tells him to leave.

At that very moment, however, Petruchio enters with the bold determination of "taming" her. He orders her food to be taken away from the table unless she thanks him; she does so, but not from the heart. Petruchio then instructs the haberdasher to produce a hat for her ... one that is obviously bigger than the fashion of the day. Katharina objects, but is quickly put in her place by Petruchio:

"I'll have no bigger, this doth fit the time,
and gentlewomen wear such caps as these.
Petruchio: When you are gentle, you shall have one too;

And not till then." (Page 130 lines 9-12)
The scene continues with Petruchio ordering the specific tailoring of Katharina's gown, including some witty exchanges with Grumio. In a speech near the end of the scene, Petruchio states that clothes do not make the man:
"Our purses shall be proud, our garments poor
For 'tis the mind that makes the body rich;
And as the sun breaks through the darkest clouds,
So honor peereth in the meanest habit."
(Page 133 lines 9-12)
Perhaps this statement leads us to believe that he sees some good in Katharina, some kindness or gentleness that is hidden beneath her volatile exterior.

In closing, he tells her that he will continue his treatment of her, his "taming" if you will, until she becomes submissive to him. "It shall be what o'clock I say it is" (Page 133 line 33).

While playing this scene, keep in mind that Petruchio is calm, collected, and master of his domain. Katharina, on the other hand, is being forced into a subservient role from every angle, and this is something she has never been forced to do. Later, when Katharina is finally tamed, she is tamed in truth. There is then no anger in her heart, for she is a woman who ultimately must speak her mind:
"My tongue will tell the anger of my heart,
Or else my heart, concealing it, will break."
(Page 130 lines 18-19)

1   *SETTING:* A room in PETRUCHIO's house.
2   *AT RISE:* Enter KATHARINA and GRUMIO.
3
4   **GRUMIO:** No, no, forsooth; I dare not, for my life.
5   **KATHARINA:** The more my wrong the more his spite
6        **appears.**
7        **What, did he marry me to famish me?**
8        **Beggars, that come unto my father's door**
9        **Upon entreaty have a present alms;**
10       **If not, elsewhere they meet with charity:**
11       **But I, who never knew how to entreat,**
12       **Am starv'd for meat, giddy for lack of sleep;**
13       **With oaths kept waking, and with brawling fed.**
14       **And that which spites me more than all these wants,**
15       **He does it under name of perfect love;**
16       **As who should say, if I should sleep or eat**
17       **'Twere deadly sickness, or else present death.**
18       **I prithee go and get me some repast;**
19       **I care not what, so it be wholesome food.**
20   **GRUMIO:** What say you to a neat's foot?
21   **KATHARINA:** 'Tis passing good: I prithee let me have it.
22   **GRUMIO:** I fear it is too choleric a meat.
23       **How say you to a fat tripe finely broil'd?**
24   **KATHARINA:** I like it well: good Grumio, fetch it me.
25   **GRUMIO:** I cannot tell; I fear 'tis choleric.
26       **What say you to a piece of beef and mustard?**
27   **KATHARINA:** A dish that I do love to feed upon.
28   **GRUMIO:** Ay, but the mustard is too hot a little.
29   **KATHARINA:** Why, then the beef, and let the mustard rest.
30   **GRUMIO:** Nay, then I will not: you shall have the mustard.
31       **Or else you get no beef of Grumio.**
32   **KATHARINA:** Then both, or one, or anything thou wilt.
33   **GRUMIO:** Why then, the mustard without the beef.
34   **KATHARINA:** Go, get thee gone, thou false deluding slave,
35       *(Beats him.)*

| | |
|---|---|
| 1 | That feed'st me with the very name of meat |
| 2 | Sorrow on thee and all the pack of you, |
| 3 | That triumph thus upon my misery! |
| 4 | Go, get thee gone, I say. |
| 5 | *(Enter PETRUCHIO with a dish of meat; and HORTENSIO.)* |
| 6 | PETRUCHIO: How fares my Kate? What, sweeting, all amort? |
| 7 | HORTENSIO: Mistress, what cheer? |
| 8 | KATHARINA: Faith, as cold as can be. |
| 9 | PETRUCHIO: Pluck up thy spirits; look cheerfully upon me. |
| 10 | Here, love; thou seest how diligent I am, |
| 11 | To dress thy meat myself and bring it thee: |
| 12 | *(Sets the dish on a table.)* |
| 13 | I am sure, sweet Kate, this kindness merits thanks. |
| 14 | What! not a word? Nay then, thou lov'st it not, |
| 15 | And all my pains is sorted to no proof. |
| 16 | Here, take away this dish. |
| 17 | KATHARINA: I pray you, let it stand. |
| 18 | PETRUCHIO: The poorest service is repaid with thanks, |
| 19 | And so shall mine, before you touch the meat. |
| 20 | KATHARINA: I thank you, sir. |
| 21 | HORTENSIO: Signior Petruchio, fie! you are to blame. |
| 22 | Come, Mistress Kate, I'll bear you company. |
| 23 | PETRUCHIO: *(Aside)* Eat it up all, Hortensio, if thou lov'st me. |
| 24 | Much good do it unto thy gentle heart! |
| 25 | Kate, eat apace: and now, my honey love, |
| 26 | Will we return unto thy father's house, |
| 27 | And revel it as bravely as the best, |
| 28 | With silken coats and caps and golden rings, |
| 29 | With ruffs and cuffs and farthingales and things; |
| 30 | With scarfs and fans and double change of bravery, |
| 31 | With amber bracelets, beads and all this knavery. |
| 32 | What! hast thou din'd? The tailor stays thy leisure, |
| 33 | To deck thy body with his ruffling treasure. |
| 34 | *(Enter TAILOR.)* |
| 35 | Come, tailor, let us see these ornaments; |

1    Lay forth the gown — *(Enter HABERDASHER.)*
2    What news with you, sir?
3    HABERDASHER: Here is the cap your worship did bespeak.
4    PETRUCHIO: Why, this was moulded on a porringer;
5       A velvet dish: fie, fie! 'tis lewd and filthy:
6       Why, 'tis a cockle or a walnutshell,
7       A knack, a toy, a trick, a baby's cap:
8       Away with it! come, let me have a bigger.
9    KATHARINA: I'll have no bigger: this doth fit the time,
10      And gentlewomen wear such caps as these.
11   PETRUCHIO: When you are gentle, you shall have one too;
12      And not till then.
13   HORTENSIO: *(Aside)* That will not be in haste.
14   KATHARINA: Why, sir, I trust I may have leave to speak,
15      And speak I will; I am no child, no babe:
16      Your betters have endur'd me say my mind,
17      And if you cannot, best you stop your ears.
18      My tongue will tell the anger of my heart,
19      Or else my heart, concealing it, will break:
20      And rather than it shall, I will be free
21      Even to the uttermost, as I please, in words.
22   PETRUCHIO: Why, thou sayst true; it is a paltry cap,
23      A custard-coffin, a bauble, a silken pie.
24      I love thee well in that thou lik'st it not.
25   KATHARINA: Love me or love me not, I like the cap,
26      And it I will have, or I will have none.
27   *(Exit HABERDASHER.)*
28   PETRUCHIO: Thy gown? why, ay: come, tailor, let us see't.
29      O mercy, God! what masquing stuff is here?
30      What's this? a sleeve? 'tis like a demi-cannon:
31      What! up and down, carv'd like an apple tart?
32      Here's snip and nip and cut and slish and slash,
33      Like to a censer in a barber's shop.
34      Why, what, i' devil's name, tailor, call'st thou this?
35   HORTENSIO: *(Aside)* I see, she's like to have neither cap

1    **nor gown.**
2    TAILOR: You bid me make it orderly and well,
3       According to the fashion and the time.
4    PETRUCHIO: Marry, and did: but if you be remember'd,
5       I did not bid you mar it to the time.
6       Go, hop me over every kennel home,
7       For you shall hop without my custom, sir.
8       I'll none of it: hence! make your best of it.
9    KATHARINA: I never saw a better-fashion'd gown,
10      More quaint, more pleasing, nor more commendable.
11      Belike you mean to make a puppet of me.
12   PETRUCHIO: Why, true; he means to make a puppet of thee.
13   TAILOR: She says your worship means to make a puppet of her.
14   PETRUCHIO: O monstrous arrogance! Thou liest, thou thread,
15      Thou thimble,
16      Thou yard, three-quarters, half-yard, quarter, nail!
17      Thou flea, thou nit, thou winter-cricket thou!
18      Brav'd in mine own house with a skein of thread!
19      Away! thou rag, thou quantity, thou remnant,
20      Or I shall so be-mete thee with thy yard
21      As thou shalt think on prating whilst thou liv'st!
22      I tell thee, I, that thou hast marr'd her gown.
23   TAILOR: Your worship is deceiv'd: the gown is made
24      Just as my master had direction.
25      Grumio gave order how it should be done.
26   GRUMIO: I gave him no order; I gave him the stuff.
27   TAILOR: But how did you desire it should be made?
28   GRUMIO: Marry, sir, with needle and thread.
29   TAILOR: But did you not request to have it cut?
30   GRUMIO: Thou hast faced many things.
31   TAILOR: I have.
32   GRUMIO: Face not me: thou hast braved many men;
33      brave not me: I will neither be faced nor braved. I say
34      unto thee, I bid thy master cut out the gown; but I did
35      not bid him cut it to pieces: ergo, thou liest.

1   TAILOR: Why, here is the note of the fashion to testify.
2   PETRUCHIO: Read it.
3   GRUMIO: The note lies in's throat if he say I said so.
4   TAILOR: "Imprimis. A loose-bodied gown."
5   GRUMIO: Master, if ever I said loose-bodied gown, sew me
6       in the skirts of it, and beat me to death with a bottom
7       of brown thread. I said, a gown.
8   PETRUCHIO: Proceed.
9   TAILOR: "With a small compassed cape."
10  GRUMIO: I confess the cape.
11  TAILOR: "With a trunk sleeve."
12  GRUMIO: I confess two sleeves.
13  TAILOR: "The sleeves curiously cut."
14  PETRUCHIO: Ay, there's the villainy.
15  GRUMIO: Error i' the bill, sir; error i' the bill. I commanded
16      the sleeves should be cut out and sewed up again; and
17      that I'll prove upon thee, though thy little finger be
18      armed in a thimble.
19  TAILOR: This is true that I say: an I had thee in place
20      where thou shouldst know it.
21  GRUMIO: I am for thee straight: take thou the bill, give
22      me thy mete-yard, and spare not me.
23  HORTENSIO: God-a-mercy, Grumio! then he shall have
24      no odds.
25  PETRUCHIO: Well, sir, in brief, the gown is not for me.
26  GRUMIO: You are i' the right, sir; 'tis for my mistress.
27  PETRUCHIO: Go, take it up unto thy master's use.
28  GRUMIO: Villain, not for thy life! take up my mistress'
29      gown for thy master's use!
30  PETRUCHIO: Why, sir, what's your conceit in that?
31  GRUMIO: O, sir, the conceit is deeper than you think for.
32      Take up my mistress' gown to his master's use!
33      O, fie, fie, fie!
34  PETRUCHIO: *(Aside)* Hortensio, say thou wilt see the
35      tailor paid.

1     *(To TAILOR)* **Go take it hence; be gone, and say no more.**
2   **HORTENSIO:** *(Aside to TAILOR)* **Tailor, I'll pay thee for**
3       **thy gown tomorrow:**
4       **Take no unkindness of his hasty words.**
5       **Away! I say; commend me to thy master.** *(Exit TAILOR.)*
6   **PETRUCHIO:** **Well, come, my Kate; we will unto your**
7       **father's,**
8       **Even in these honest mean habiliments.**
9       **Our purses shall be proud, our garments poor**
10      **For 'tis the mind that makes the body rich;**
11      **And as the sun breaks through the darkest clouds,**
12      **So honour peereth in the meanest habit.**
13      **What is the jay more precious than the lark**
14      **Because his feathers are more beautiful?**
15      **Or is the adder better than the eel**
16      **Because his painted skin contents the eye?**
17      **O, no, good Kate; neither art thou the worse**
18      **For this poor furniture and mean array.**
19      **If thou account'st it shame, lay it on me;**
20      **And therefore frolic: we will hence forthwith,**
21      **To feast and sport us at thy father's house.**
22      **Go, call my men, and let us straight to him;**
23      **And bring our horses unto Long-lane end;**
24      **There will we mount, and thither walk on foot.**
25      **Let's see; I think 'tis now some seven o'clock,**
26      **And well we may come there by dinnertime.**
27   **KATHARINA:** **I dare assure you, sir, 'tis almost two;**
28      **And 'twill be supper time ere you come there.**
29   **PETRUCHIO:** **It shall be seven ere I go to horse.**
30      **Look, what I speak, or do, or think to do,**
31      **You are still crossing it. Sirs, let 't alone:**
32      **I will not go today; and ere I do,**
33      **It shall be what o'clock I say it is.**
34   **HORTENSIO:** **Why, so this gallant will command the sun.**
35     *(Exit.)*

# The Taming of the Shrew
## Act IV, Scene 5

**Characters:** Petruchio, Katharina, Hortensio, Vincentio

This scene occurs toward the end of the play. In order to fully comprehend this scene, one must understand what has transpired thus far and know about the characters.

Briefly stated, Petruchio, a gentleman from Verona, has come to Padua in hopes of finding a wife. He is a man of extreme confidence; furthermore, he is witty, clever, intelligent, and highly adventurous. Earlier in the play, his friend Hortensio told him about Katharina, a single woman from a wealthy family, and this prospect intrigued Petruchio. To add fuel to the fire, she is a volatile woman with a sharp tongue and hot temper.

The possibility of a match with this woman fascinates Petruchio, and he is consumed with the idea of "taming" her; it would prove to be his ultimate challenge. Throughout the play, he realizes that making Katharina submissive will be no easy task, but the process of taming her excites him even more, thus driving him forward. Indeed, had he wanted a calm woman, he would have sought the hand of her sister, Bianca.

Petruchio has married Katharina and taken her to his house in Padua. In an earlier scene, he has threatened to strike her (Act II, Scene 1), though he does not. She recognizes his strength and iron will and responds to the threat accordingly by temporarily backing down. In another scene (Act IV, Scene 3), he is outfitting her in the latest fashions and instructs the haberdasher to create a hat larger than she wants. When she protests, she claims that "gentlewomen wear such caps as these." His response is quick, curt, and to the point: "When you are gentle, you shall have one too; and not till then." (Page 130 lines 11 & 12)

In a previous scene, Petruchio promises Katharina that he will not

134

ease up on his quest of taming her; he will continue to pursue his intentions of making her subservient. As a matter of fact, he ends the third scene in this act by stating, "It shall be what o'clock I say it is." In other words, she will and must agree with him on every issue, no matter if it is true or not.

At this point in the play, Katharina is finally and completely tamed. Petruchio, Katharina, and his friend Hortensio are on their way with a few servants to Baptista's house in Padua. Petruchio states that the moon is very bright; in response, Katharina says that it is not the moon, but the sun. Petruchio then clearly states that it will be what he says it is, or they will return home at once without visiting Padua. Katharina realizes that if she ever wants peace she must make herself a pleasant companion and agree with what her husband says; she relents and says that it is the sun and will be whatever Petruchio sees fit.

"... be it moon, or sun, or what you please.
And if you please to call it a rush-candle,
Henceforth I vow it shall be so for me."
(Page 137 lines 17-19)

During their trip, they happen upon Vincentio, an older man with a wild temper. Playing the charade, Petruchio addresses him as a lovely young girl; Katharina, aware of her duties as the "tamed shrew," quickly responds that she is a lovely young virgin. Ever in control, Petruchio states that his wife must be mistaken — this is indeed an old, wrinkled, and withered man, not a lovely young virgin like she said. She quickly replies:

"Pardon, old father, my mistaking eyes,
That have been so bedazzled with the sun
That everything I look on seemeth green:
Now I perceive thou art a reverend father;
Pardon, I pray thee, for my mad mistaking."
(Page 138 lines 18-22)

This moment, it can be argued, is the climax of Petruchio's quest. It is the moment at which the shrew is tamed. In other words, the formerly unhappy Katharina discovers how to be happy. Her husband's firmness and steadfastness have turned her into a reasonable woman. Petruchio, from this point on, becomes a better and more reasonable husband as well. He no longer will starve her or keep her from rest, and he will no longer strike his servants or shout and swear noisily. His quest is satisfied and completed, and he can now live in harmony and happiness with his wife.

It is amusing to note that while talking to Vincentio, Petruchio discovers that they could be related because Vincentio's son, Lucentio, is planning to marry Katharina's sister. Hortensio ends the scene with remarks that he, too, will tame his widow as Petruchio has tamed Katharina.

1    *SETTING:* A public road.
2    *AT RISE:*   Enter PETRUCHIO, KATHARINA, HORTENSIO,
3       and Servants.
4    **PETRUCHIO: Come on, i' God's name; once more toward**
5       **our father's.**
6       **Good Lord, how bright and goodly shines the moon!**
7    **KATHARINA: The moon! the sun: it is not moonlight now.**
8    **PETRUCHIO: I say it is the moon that shines so bright.**
9    **KATHARINA: I know it is the sun that shines so bright.**
10   **PETRUCHIO: Now, by my mother's son, and that's myself,**
11      **It shall be the moon, or star, or what I list,**
12      **Or ere I journey to your father's house.**
13      **Go one and fetch our horses back again.**
14      **Evermore cross'd and cross'd; nothing but cross'd!**
15   **HORTENSIO: Say as he says, or we shall never go.**
16   **KATHARINA: Forward, I pray, since we have come so far,**
17      **And be it moon, or sun, or what you please.**
18      **An if you please to call it a rush-candle,**
19      **Henceforth I vow it shall be so for me.**
20   **PETRUCHIO: I say it is the moon.**
21   **KATHARINA: I know it is the moon.**
22   **PETRUCHIO: Nay, then you lie; it is the blessed sun.**
23   **KATHARINA: Then God be bless'd, it is the blessed sun;**
24      **But sun it is not when you say it is not,**
25      **And the moon changes even as your mind.**
26      **What you will have it nam'd, even that it is;**
27      **And so, it shall be so for Katharine.**
28   **HORTENSIO: Petruchio, go thy ways; the field is won.**
29   **PETRUCHIO: Well, forward, forward! thus the bowl should**
30      **run,**
31      **And not unluckily against the bias.**
32      **But soft! what company is coming here?**
33      *(Enter VINCENTIO, in a traveling dress.)*
34      *(To VINCENTIO)* **Good morrow, gentle mistress: where**
35      **away?**

1    Tell me, sweet Kate, and tell me truly too,
2    Hast thou beheld a fresher gentlewoman?
3    Such war of white and red within her cheeks!
4    What stars do spangle heaven with such beauty,
5    As those two eyes become that heavenly face?
6    Fair lovely maid, once more good day to thee.
7    Sweet Kate, embrace her for her beauty's sake.
8  HORTENSIO: A' will make the man mad, to make a woman
9       of him.
10 KATHARINA: Young budding virgin, fair and fresh and sweet,
11      Whither away, or where is thy abode?
12      Happy the parents of so fair a child;
13      Happier the man, whom favourable stars
14      Allot thee for his lovely bedfellow!
15 PETRUCHIO: Why, how now, Kate! I hope thou art not mad:
16      This is a man, old, wrinkled, faded, wither'd,
17      And not a maiden, as thou sayst he is.
18 KATHARINA: Pardon, old father, my mistaking eyes,
19      That have been so bedazzled with the sun
20      That everything I look on seemeth green:
21      Now I perceive thou art a reverend father;
22      Pardon, I pray thee, for my mad mistaking.
23 PETRUCHIO: Do, good old grandsire; and withal make
24      known
25      Which way thou travellest: if along with us,
26      We shall be joyful of thy company.
27 VINCENTIO: Fair sir, and you my merry mistress,
28      That with your strange encounter much amaz'd me,
29      My name is called Vincentio; my dwelling, Pisa;
30      And bound I am to Padua, there to visit
31      A son of mine, which long I have not seen.
32 PETRUCHIO: What is his name?
33 VINCENTIO: Lucentio, gentle sir.
34 PETRUCHIO: Happily met; the happier for thy son.
35      And now by law, as well as reverend age,

| | |
|---|---|
| 1 | I may entitle thee my loving father: |
| 2 | The sister to my wife, this gentlewoman, |
| 3 | Thy son by this hath married. Wonder not, |
| 4 | Nor be not griev'd: she is of good esteem, |
| 5 | Her dowry wealthy, and of worthy birth; |
| 6 | Beside, so qualified as may beseem |
| 7 | The spouse of any noble gentleman. |
| 8 | Let me embrace with old Vincentio; |
| 9 | And wander we to see thy honest son, |
| 10 | Who will of thy arrival be full joyous. |
| 11 | VINCENTIO: But is this true? or is it else your pleasure, |
| 12 | Like pleasant travellers, to break a jest |
| 13 | Upon the company you overtake? |
| 14 | HORTENSIO: I do assure thee, father, so it is. |
| 15 | PETRUCHIO: Come, go along, and see the truth hereof; |
| 16 | For our first merriment hath made thee jealous. |
| 17 | *(Exit all but HORTENSIO.)* |
| 18 | HORTENSIO: Well, Petruchio, this has put me in heart. |
| 19 | Have to my widow! and if she be froward, |
| 20 | Then hast thou taught Hortensio to be untoward. |
| 21 | *(He exits.)* |
| 22 | |
| 23 | |
| 24 | |
| 25 | |
| 26 | |
| 27 | |
| 28 | |
| 29 | |
| 30 | |
| 31 | |
| 32 | |
| 33 | |
| 34 | |
| 35 | |

# About the Editor

**Michael Wilson,** editor of the original *Scenes from Shakespeare* as well as this book, graduated from Cal State University, Chico in 1974 with a degree in English. He received his teaching credential the following year from Chico, and did graduate work at Fresno State and Fresno Pacific College. He has been teaching in the Visalia Unified School District for twenty-three years and has taught theater arts for the past eighteen years. He currently teaches three levels of drama, along with American Literature and Advanced Composition/Grammar. He directs and produces plays for Golden West High School and has directed over fifty plays and musicals thus far.

He is also a professional musician, playing guitar for a ten-piece soul, funk, and classic rock band named Run 4 Cover. He has performed in different parts of California, Las Vegas, and at Super Bowl XXIII.

# Order Form

**Meriwether Publishing Ltd.**
P.O. Box 7710
Colorado Springs, CO 80933
Telephone: (719) 594-4422
Website: www.meriwetherpublishing.com

*Please send me the following books:*

**More Scenes From Shakespeare #BK-B230 $12.95**
edited by Michael Wilson
*Twenty cuttings for acting and directing practice*

**Scenes From Shakespeare #BK-B120**           $12.95
edited by Michael Wilson
*Fifteen cuttings for the classroom*

**Scenes and Monologs from the Best**           $14.95
**New Plays #BK-B140**
edited by Roger Ellis
*An anthology of new American plays*

**The Scenebook for Actors #BK-B177**           $15.95
by Norman A. Bert
*Collection of great monologs and dialogs for auditions*

**Playing Contemporary Scenes #BK-B100 $15.95**
edited by Gerald Lee Ratliff
*Thirty-one famous scenes and how to play them*

**Winning Monologs for Young Actors**           $14.95
**#BK-B127**
by Peg Kehret
*Honest-to-life monologs for young actors*

**Theatre Games and Beyond #BK-B217**           $15.95
by Amiel Schotz
*A creative approach for performers*

These and other fine Meriwether Publishing books are available at
your local bookstore or direct from the publisher. Use the handy
order form on this page.

Name: _____

Organization name: _____

Address: _____

City: _____ State: _____

Zip: _____ Phone: _____

❏  **Check Enclosed**

❏  **Visa or MasterCard #** _____

Signature: _____     *Expiration*
                                     *Date:* _____
       *(required for Visa/MasterCard orders)*

**COLORADO RESIDENTS:** Please add 3% sales tax.
**SHIPPING:** Include $2.75 for the first book and 50¢ for each additional book ordered.

❏  *Please send me a copy of your complete catalog of books and plays.*